PERSPECTIVE: AFRICA

Volume 3.1

September 2016

PUBLISHED BY:

Perspective Publications
http://perspective-publications.com

Executive Editor

Leigh Barrett

Website: http://www.perspective-publications.org

Email: editor@perspective-publications.org

Twitter: @SVillage01

Perspective: Africa is available in full color, black/white, and digital versions

ISBN: 9781537486185

All content in Perspective: Africa (Volume 3, Edition 1 / September 2016)
is used with permission and is under copyright to each
respective contributor and/or his/her assigns.
Perspective: Africa is a quarterly journal, distributed internationally.
Subscriptions available.

Executive Produced by Skambha Village:
info@skambha-village.org
For further information, or for any questions, please contact:
info@skambha-village.org

Published by:
Perspective Publications
Reg No: 9175434225
8 Brakkekloof, Harrington Road
Fish Hoek, Cape Town, 7975
(027)79-815-0659

Table of Contents

From the Executive Editor

Leigh Barrett

New publications, especially those focusing on current affairs, news, and especially humanitarian issues as this one does, rarely make it past the starting gate in this world where people would rather buy the soundbite tabloids at the supermarket check-out.

While Sisyphus has nothing on us at Perspective Publications, the ability to continue getting these important stories out can only succeed through you, the reader, supporting the efforts of our exceptionally talented contributors who keep stepping up to the plate - and consistently, to stretch the metaphor, knocking it out the park. So, a heartfelt thank you!

IN THIS ISSUE:

The drama unfolding at the Wild Coast, a story which we began in the March 2016 issue and will continue to follow, took some dramatic turns since you were last here - and this time directly and personally impacts one of our writers, John GI Clarke, who has been serializing the story through our pages. The latest developments are an alarming look at how far a power-monger will go to avoid dealing with the consequences of his actions - even where those actions have a deleterious effect on people with whom he has never bothered to meet.

Also, photo features from two of the world's finest photojournalists: Anthony Karen, who submitted some extraordinary photographs from Somalia, and Mario Cruz, in collaboration with FotoEvidence, who focused in on the children of Senegal, and the desperate situation of the Talibes.

Mandy Tomson attacks, with her usual

aplomb, various news stories that have attracted headlines, and gives us another way to look at them. We hope Mandy's missives from the Wild Side will become a regular column from her.

Mandy also contributed a superb article on an issue that is a hot topic in America as well as South Africa - black lives matter - should inspire thought and discussion. The article is posted on the Perspective blog, and you are invited to add your thoughts to that discussion.

This issue covers a wide array of topics, which more than reaches our goal at Perspective: to offer you, the reader, the widest views of the continent, to garner understanding of the issues, the people, and the diverse cultures of Africa, and to allow anyone with a voice to assist in informing you about this most diverse and fascinating land.

We thank all the contributors for helping make this an interesting, informative, and educational read.

Thank you for your continued support,

Leigh

The Horn's Mayday

by Leigh Barrett

The ancient city of Mogadishu has a profoundly rich history. The original hunter-gatherer tribes mingled with agrarian tribes and formed an Arab aristocracy that ruled between the 10th and 16th centuries. An exceptionally important trading empire, Mogadishu, as a Sultanate and then as the country known today as Somalia, dominated the gold trade at the time, minted its own coin, and left an architectural legacy that earned the nickname, White Pearl of the Indian Ocean.

Somali traders established a colony in Mozambique to mine gold found there, and developed regional trade that made it a trading empire. In 1871, the Sultan of Zanzibar opened the door to the Italians by leasing them Mogadishu's port. After that, it rapidly became one of Italy's colonies.

Under Italian rule from 1889 – 1936, the Italians bought the port in 1905, and made it the capital city.

Mussolini considered 'Somaliland' the crown jewel in the Italian colonial empire, and saw the strategic importance of its location in launching into Africa and the Second Italo-Abyssinian War from 1935 – 36. That resulted in Italy occupying poorly equipped Ethiopia, a move considered the peak of Mussolini's popularity.

By the time the Second World War erupted, Italian Somaliland accommodated over 50,000 Italians with 20,000 living in Mogadishu, comprising around 40% of the city's population.

All men and boys able to carry a spear go to Addis Ababa. Every married man will bring his wife to cook and wash for him. Every unmarried man will bring any unmarried woman he can find to cook and wash for him. Women with babies, the blind, and those too aged and infirm to carry a spear are excused. Anyone found at home after receiving this order will be hanged. - Selassie's Mobilization Order

A series of treaties passed Somalia between Italian, British and United Nations rule until 1960, when the British-controlled British Somaliland, united with Italian-controlled Somaliland, to form an independent Republic.

As the colonials left Somalis to govern themselves, the generations of conflict had left their mark and when President Abdirashad Ali Shermarke was assassinated in 1969, followed by a military coup the day after his funeral, things rapidly went from bad to devastating.

The revolutionary army suspended the constitution, banned political parties, dissolved Parliament, and started a nationalization program to try and restore Somalia's importance in the Arab world, while their paranoia grew into oppressive actions which saw the execution of many opponents to the regime. As the government became more unpopular and discontent grew, various resistance movements sprang up, and civil war was inevitable.

The United Nations stepped in to try and stabilize the situation, placing peacekeepers in the country in 1992 and forming UNOSOM to secure humanitarian efforts. The UN involvement was seen as a slight to the government's independence, and various violent battles between government forces and UN peacekeepers ensued, including the Battle of Mogadishu in 1993, which resulted in peacekeepers being withdrawn completely.

From 2000 to 2004, the internationally recognized government of Somalia was the Transitional National Government, which in 2004 was replaced by the Transitional Federal Government (TFG). The TFG re-established Somalia's military, and in 2006, after Sharia Law was instituted by the Islamic Courts Union (ICU) a group that had taken control of most of the southern part of the country, drove the fundamentalists out of Mogadishu

This pivotal move meant the federal government controlled the capital and most of the country for the first time since 1991.

The ICU, splintering into various smaller groups of varying strength, dissolved, but the most radical element, Al-Shabaab continued the fight, with bloody battles forcing the Ethiopians and UN to leave, and only the ill-equipped African Union troops remaining to protect the Somalis.

A conference in 2008 saw the beginning of the long journey to peace, brokered by the UN. Parliament expanded to accommodate some of the rebel groups, and a new offensive to take control of the southern half of the country was launched with the assistance of the African Union. But, while the splinter groups from the ICU were happy to join the government, Al-Shabaab resisted all efforts and continue to deploy traditional terrorism tactics ("hit-and-run") to keep pecking away at the young peace of the country. Mogadishu now has a plan to reconstruct itself, creating new housing and infrastructure and stabilizing the country economically, despite Al-Shabaab's best efforts to disrupt their chances.

LATEST

Mid-August saw Somali forces, assisted by US-led advisers, attacked an Al-Shabaab group in southern Somalia killing several members. Al-Shabaab raise funds by operating checkpoints where they "tax" residents and merchants moving through the area.

In March 2016, a group of males, ranging in age from 13 years to old men, were captured by government forces. The youngest boys explained that they had been promised an education if they fought for the militants.

Faced with grinding poverty, groups like Al-Shabaab prey on children as young as 10, using their desperation to create a better life for themselves and their families as a recruitment tool. Militants also force parents to give up their children, and many families live in fear once their sons reach fighting age. The very places families send their children to be educated – schools at local mosques – have become target-rich recruitment zones for Al-Shabaab. Under Somali law, as well as international laws and conventions, enlisting child soldiers is a war crime.

Photo: AMISOM Public Information

CATHEDRAL OF MOGADISHU

The Italians built the magnificent Mogadishu Cathedral in 1928 and over the ensuing years of conflict, it has been the site of various attacks: the final and most devastating being in 2008, when much of the cathedral was destroyed by Islamic fundamentalists. Despite the ruined building, it has remained the protective site for many internally displaced people who set up tents and makeshift shelters in the grounds.

The Roman Catholic Diocese of Mogadiscio has announced plans to repair the building, but with only around 100 Catholics (and possibly 70% of whom are foreign aid workers) in a country that is 99.8% Muslim, it is difficult to say whether the Cathedral will ever see a return to its former glory.

Photo: AMISOM Public Information

Photo: AMISOM Public Information

Below: Mogadishu's Peace Garden

Photo: AMISOM Public Information

Striving for development: Since the early 1990s, various militant groups used Mogadishu stadium as their base of operations. Al-Shabaab banned sporting events when they laid siege to the city in 2008, but after the Somali National Army recaptured the city in 2011 the federal government, with assistance from China, renovated the stadium.

Photo: AMISOM Public Information

Photo: AMISOM Public Information

Courtesy: Office of the Special Representative of the Secretary-General for Children and Armed Conflict

Read the report by scanning this QR code, or visiting the Perspective Publications website Links page:

Somalia

Photo Essay by Anthony Karen
Text by Anthony Karen and Leigh Barrett

Above: A Somali refugee at the Badbaado IDP Camp.

Badbaado and Jowhar IDP Camps

Located just outside Mogadishu, the Badbaado camp was formed after the 2011 drought that devastated much of East Africa, and has since been refuge to those fleeing the violence. It currently houses around 30,000 refugees. Over the ensuing years, numerous reports of abuses against the refugees have reached the media. Those running the camp have been accused of working for the militia and reports of rape, beatings, refused access to food and medical care, and reprisals for those who complain, appear to be common and keep the displaced people at the mercy of those who control access, according to a Human Rights Watch report. Less refugees and more hostages, the understandable anger towards those in authority mingles with the despair of those who have no choices left.

Children also struggle to receive an education which is crucial if the country is to ever get past its violent history, and while some schools receive donations from international NGO's, it's not enough to cover the costs, resulting in many schools closing down. The cycle of history and poverty, which often finds direction in violence, appears doomed to repeat itself.

Jowhar camp is in the town of Jowhar, a joint administrative capital north of Mogadishu.

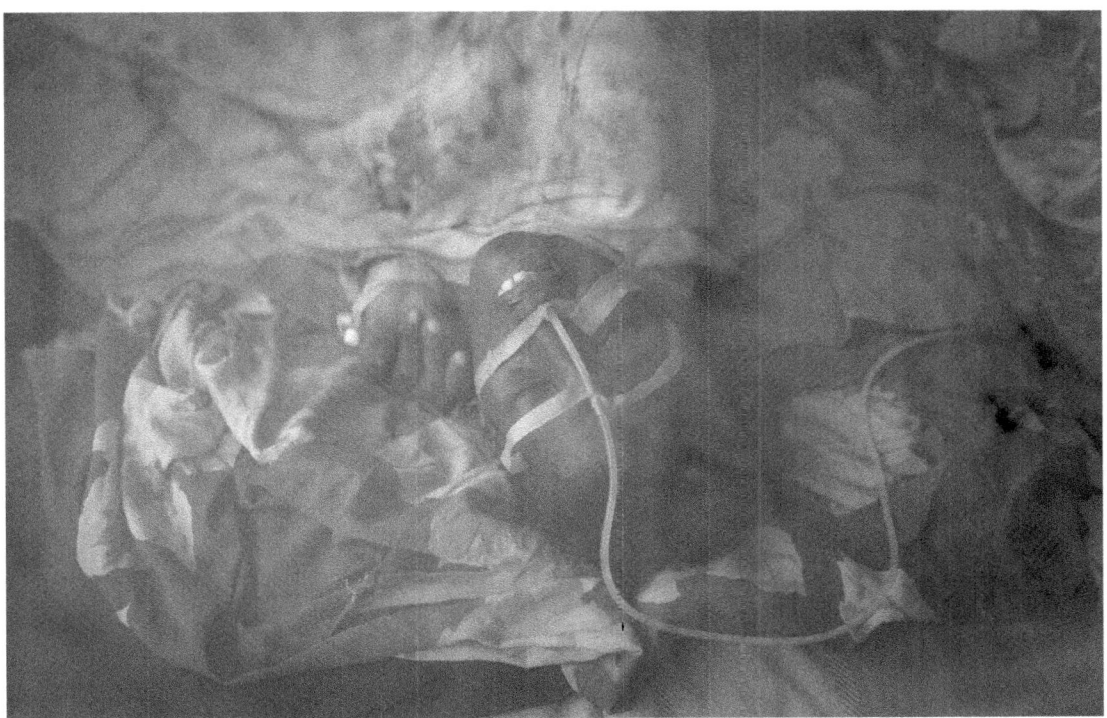

Above: A ten-year-old boy lies in a coma at the Banadir Hospital in Mogadishu, Somalia. The boy was shot in the head three months prior during a battle between TFG forces and Al-Shabab militants in the capital city of Mogadishu.

BANADIR MOTHER & CHILD HOSPITAL

Built in 1977 as part of a Chinese development partnership with Somalia, the hospital is one of the few remaining medical centers still operating, and the only one specializing in treating children affected by drought, diarrhea, and cholera.

A picture of the humanitarian crisis the hospital dealt with in 2011 can be seen in the WHO report by scanning this QR code. Most recently, in March 2016, a fire gutted the pediatric drug store of the hospital, adding further stress to a facility that received due credit for staying operational through Somalia's civil war.

MEDINA HOSPITAL

The other major hospital focuses on trauma and emergency maternal medicine, struggling with a lack of modern equipment, as well as religious objections by some patients' families who would sometimes rely on the "will of God", rather than modern medicine. Women are bound by the will of their husband or father, creating a difficult situation for medical professionals who spend valuable time trying to convince them to approve of relatively simple procedures such as Caesarian section. If a woman arrives alone, valuable time can be spent locating an accountable male; time which can prove fatal.

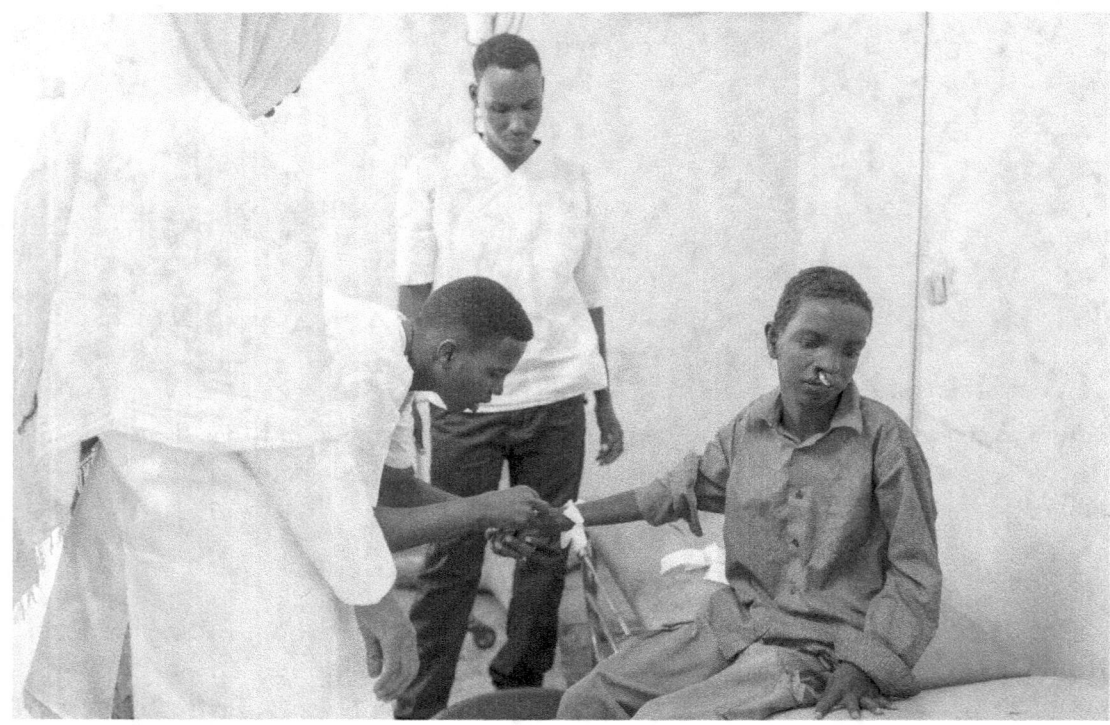

Anthony Karen: "I came across this young boy in an IDP (Internally Displaced Persons) camp in Mogadishu, Somalia while documenting another project. Due to my affiliation with Smile Train, I was able to help facilitate his corrective surgery with the help of the head surgeon at Medina Hospital in Mogadishu. This image was taken an hour before his surgery."

Above: A prisoner accused of murder at the Central prison of Mogadishu, Hodan District, Somalia.

Mogadishu Central Prison

Common in many prisons globally, the growing number of prisoners in Mogadishu's Central Prison comes with decreased sanitary conditions, outbreaks of diseases like dysentery and cholera, made worse by the hot climate of Somalia. Visits in 2013 by the cabinet ministers responsible for the prison have resulted in concrete action taken to increase services to the prisoners, including clean water, medical treatment, and workshops that will increase skill levels to prepare prisoners for employment on release.

Above: The Fish Abattoir Market in the Hamar Weyne district, Mogadishu, Somalia.

Hamar-weyne

One of Mogadishu's 16 districts is Hamar-weyne, said to have been established over 1,000 years ago. Several ancient buildings have been found as having used milk as mortar, instead of water and cement.

Since 2005, massive efforts by SAACID and UN_HABITAT have been underway to re-build this oldest of the city's districts, including the famous Barduuro Market. Founded in 1972, it was closed after 1991, and reopened in 2009. It currently accommodates 60 vibrant businesses. In 2016, it hosted an event to revive the culture of the city, perhaps an indication of the people's need to honor the extraordinary cosmopolitan and cultural heritage that is Mogadishu, despite the constant efforts of Al-Shabaab to keep making war on their country. The fish market is also a bustling venue.

The much reported piracy off the coast of Somalia developed largely after the collapse of the government and the intrusion by international commercial fishing fleets. Somali waters were being plundered and fishermen, feeling their livelihoods were under threat, began demanding "taxes" from the ships. The dumping of toxic and nuclear waste in that region by European Union ships mostly from Italy, Denmark, and Germany, and sometimes also transporting hazardous waste from Australia, combined with the discovery of unidentified skin diseases and malformed babies, left the Somali people with little recourse to combat both extreme threats and many used piracy as a means to fight for attention and survival.

Above: A TFG (Transitional Federal Government solider) on patrol in the Hamar Weyne district, Mogadishu, Somalia.

Since it costs around $2.50 per tonne to dump it off Africa's coast, compared to $250 per tonne in Europe, the abuse of Africa's least developed by the world's most developed nations is a story familiar to all Africans, but it is the piracy that draws the most attention, not least because it makes for a good Hollywood blockbuster in a way a baby with life threatening birth defects does not.

With the continued growth of Somalia over the last 3 years, levels of piracy have dropped dramatically, and the growth in the economy and food markets seem to be directly linked.

Anthony Karen is a photojournalist based in New York. Over the years, Anthony has worked on several long-term projects, including extensive documentation of the Ku Klux Klan, with several books and exhibitions produced internationally. Anthony served in the US Marine Corps and has traveled extensively, volunteering on numerous international medical missions. His charitable affiliations include Hospice, Smile Train, Surgical Volunteers International and the Humane Society.

An officer in charge of the jail facilities at a police station in Mogadishu, Somalia.

Above: A young refugee on the grounds of the Cathedral of Mogadishu.

Below: Displaced children living within the Badbaado IDP Camp.

Black Lives Should Matter –
In America And Africa

by Mandy Tomson

The Black Lives Matter movement in the United States is gaining increasing momentum and interracial support as Americans finally confront the toxic mix of black poverty, police officers' racial paranoia, and the indisputable fact that black men are far more likely to die during an interaction with the police than whites.

Previously, many questioned the often hostile, uncooperative behaviour of the young black men involved. Why didn't he just put his hands up when asked? Why didn't he stop running? Why didn't he stop advancing on the police? Why didn't he just do as he was told and litigate the details later? Two recent cases point to the vulnerability of black American men regardless of what they do.

Philando Castile did everything by the book. When the police pulled him over for a broken tail light, he immediately complied. He behaved politely, showed his hands and explained to the police officer that he had a gun along with a license to carry said gun. Clearly, he wasn't planning to shoot it out with the cops otherwise he wouldn't have let them know in advance that he had a gun. The cop asked him for his driver's license and he reached for it and was executed in front of his girlfriend and child.

His girlfriend who was simply a passenger and had done absolutely nothing wrong was handcuffed and taken to the police station. On what grounds?

A black behavioural therapist trying to rein in his errant (white) autistic patient lies in the street, legs apart and hands in the air, while his patient sits muttering and playing with a toy truck.

The black man shouts to the police that he is a therapist and his patient has no gun and is simply playing with a toy truck. Incredibly, a police officer shoots him in the leg. The victim says, "why did you shoot me?!" The white cop says, "I don't know!"

Unfortunately, both victims overestimated the rationality of the police officers and underestimated their instinctive racial paranoia.

So far, most of the proposed solutions involve more detailed use-of-force guidelines. However, the existing ones have already become a reliable shield behind which police get away with murder.

While living in Los Angeles in the 1990s and early 2000s, I recall the case of a tiny, homeless, demented 80-year-old black woman who stood outside a supermarket, waving a screwdriver and ranting incoherently. (There is a disproportionately large percentage of homeless people in Southern California by virtue of the temperate weather – it is far easier to survive winter there than in the icy, snowy climes of the East Coast. Most of the homeless are mentally ill and/or substance abusers and/or Vietnam vets). A bunch of burly cops arrived and apparently could think of no way to resolve the situation except by pumping this tiny, fragile old lady full of bullets – ultimately and incredibly, ruled "a justifiable homicide" on account of her "brandishing a deadly weapon" which caused them to "fear for their lives." Since they met the written use-of-force guidelines, they were acquitted.

If these police officers were at a family barbecue and their demented great-grandmother picked up a knife and waved it around, you can bet the relatives would find a way to resolve the situation without opening fire. "Hey, you distract her from the front, and I'll grab her from behind…" No one would say, "Let me go inside the house, get my gun and shoot her."

These elaborately technical use-of-force guidelines have eliminated the umbrella of context and commonsense and allowed police officers to get away with murdering black people across the United States.

The black community needs to take some responsibility for not cooperating with the police: having lived for many years in a predominantly black Los Angeles neighbourhood controlled by the Shoreline Crips, I can testify that in my gang- and drug-infested neighbourhood, people would mourn their loved ones at funerals, knowing full well the identity of the killers, but refuse to say who did it; this, in turn, fuelled anger and resentment within the local police force who felt their attempts to secure justice for the victims were continually frustrated by the victims' own loved ones. However, the police need to take responsibility for being paranoid and trigger-happy under any and all circumstances that involve black men no matter what the context, creating distrust in the very communities they are trying to serve.

It is also imperative to remember that amid this extreme focus on violent encounters between police and black people, and Donald Trump's stereotypical rhetoric, it is easy to conclude that all black Americans are unemployed and poor, and/or gangsters, in constant conflict with the police. The reality is that 74 percent of black Americans are working, middle and upper class; they live in safe, integrated neighbourhoods, flourish socially and economically, and have limited contact with the police. A black man driving a brand-new Mercedes Benz in West Los Angeles attracts zero attention from the police because it is an affluent, integrated area and they have seen plenty of black people in Bentleys, Teslas and Rolls Royces; a black man driving a brand-new Mercedes Benz in a poor, gang-plagued neighbourhood like South Central Los Angeles will find himself followed by the police who are looking to pull him over on some traffic-related technicality. Why? Because the cops suspect that either the Mercedes is stolen or the man is from West LA and is visiting their part of town to score drugs; they don't want to let some rich yuppie help sustain the demand for the drugs that are ruining the community they police. Facts and context are everything in these matters.

What the Black Lives Matter movement still needs to address is the prosecutorial dimension of this problem which is far more sinister and impactful than any encounter in the streets: after all, it isn't trigger-happy patrol officers who determine someone's prison sentence. A white woman holds her estranged husband hostage for hours, shoots five times and hits him three times, and serves four years; a black woman in Florida fires a warning shot in a confrontation with her estranged, abusive partner and gets 20 years for endangering her children who could have been injured (but weren't).

American prosecutors routinely seek maximum charges and sentences for black defendants, especially those whose limited financial resources force them to depend on an overworked public defender for their legal representation. (Even middle-class Americans would not be able to afford a private lawyer for a criminal defence that would cost well over $100 000 – approximately R1.4 million – without going bankrupt). The racist application of the law results in the disproportionately long-term imprisonment of millions of black people, aided by drug laws from Ronald Reagan's presidency that punish possession

of crack (cooked cocaine, mostly used by poor people) with far heavier sentences than possession of powder cocaine (used mainly by white yuppies). Prosecutors also routinely use taxpayer money to resist DNA tests in older cases that could exonerate convicts. Why are they so afraid of scientific evidence if they believe the convictions were justified?

America has only begun to scratch the surface of these problems that have festered for generations. However, more use-of-force guidelines are definitely not the answer unless they specifically bow to commonsense and context.

What about black lives on our continent? Every day, black defendants show up in South African courts with bruises, cuts and assorted injuries from being assaulted by police officers who simply deny the accusations. Those arrested cannot prove which police officers assaulted them and so nothing happens. This problem could be solved by placing CCTV in every cell and interrogation room but nothing is done. Nevertheless, these South African accused criminals are lucky by African standards – at least they make it to court: across the continent, detainees simply disappear, their mutilated bodies occasionally discovered weeks later. There is little to zero accountability. As Zimbabweans rise up against Robert Mugabe's disastrous rule, our television screens are filled with images of police officers dragging citizens out of their homes and beating them senseless.

As noted by South African journalist and author, Sandile Memela: "When a black man violates the rights of another black man, nobody cares. It happens so often that it has become a way of life. But when a white man violates a black man, brouha-ha breaks out."

The incompetence of the South African police force combined with the willingness of magistrates and judges to grant bail have depleted faith in the criminal justice system. Vigilante mob violence in South Africa has become informal sharia law – so routine that it doesn't even make the front pages: black South Africans brutally execute their own on the basis of rumour, often with the complicit passivity of the police. If a mob of white South Africans killed a black South African, it would be front-page news, police officers would suddenly experience an attack of diligence and arrests would be made amid a furore about the need to eliminate racism.

Why is black-on-black slavery, exploitation, torture and oppression in Africa routinely accepted amid an inordinate focus on crimes and exploitation committed by whites?

The legacy of European colonialism and South Africa's apartheid policy understandably generated a suspicious focus on the conduct and motives of Western nations and whites – unfortunately to the exclusion of more relevant contemporary realities. White people constitute approximately 9% of South Africa's population and 1% of Africa's population: they punch above their weight economically on account of the legacy of privilege bestowed on them by colonialism and apartheid, but they hold no political power and no longer control the fate of African countries, so fixating on them does little to improve the quality of life on our beloved continent.

In South Africa which has the continent's largest number of whites, the rising level of frustration with poverty and crime is expressing itself in irrational, often racially charged tangents that can only poison the country further backward.

Whites are now feeling targeted by the ruling African National Congress which blames apartheid for the nation's persistent racial and class inequality rather than focusing on its own failures and what is possible in the here and now. Racist whites, drowning in media reports about corruption and assorted chicanery, cry "I told you blacks can't run the country," and some react with defiantly vile outbursts on social media, while progressive whites feel helpless to positively influence the outcome of events.

Instead of focusing on the thieves in government who are stealing their futures, we are now seeing an obsessive, militant focus on "whiteness" and the symbols of colonialism and apartheid among black "born-free" university students. Black South African students are focusing their energy and militancy on demanding the removal of statues of dead white racists and land thieves which will have zero impact on the quality of African lives in the 21st century; they also want free tertiary education, despite the massive deficiencies in South Africa's basic education system which is supposed to serve everyone – not just those bright enough to get into university.

University of Cape Town professor of sociology, Xolela Mangcu, recounted his acute embarrassment at participating on a panel with progressive visiting academics from the University of California, Berkeley. Bullying black students physically got in his face and "hurled insults at the panel-

Photo: HelenSTB

Photo: Leigh Barrett

Top Left: The defaced statue of Louis Botha, First South African Prime Minister (1910-1919). Cape Town, 2015.

Top Right: After the 2015 "Rhodes Must Fall" student protests, the nose on the Cecil John Rhodes statue at the Rhodes Memorial, Cape Town, was damaged.

Below: The statue of Cecil John Rhodes at the University of Cape Town is removed after the 2015 protests. Rhodes served as Prime Minister of the Cape Colony from 1890 - 1896.

Photo: Desmond Bowles

lists as white people who were there to tell black people what to do."

A black student leader appearing on Judge Dennis Davis' television show, "Judge for Yourself," sanctimoniously announced that she rejected "whiteness in all its forms." Apparently, all white people are essentially the same – innately privileged, racist and inherently incapable of progressive thought and action. This assertion is reiterated by intellectually confused, guilt-stricken whites like writer Gillian Schutte who opines that white babies are racist in utero. Of course apartheid gave white people privileges: that was its raison d'être. It was the world's biggest affirmative-action program for whites who were so "superior" that they needed whole professions reserved for them to ensure their economic success. However, it is tragic to see black university students favour reactive bigotry as some sort of solution to the irritating, continued existence of white South Africans and their inherited privilege.

Bigotry is a mode of reasoning: whether it is racism, sexism, anti-Semitism, Islamophobia, homophobia, zenophobia or tribalism, it involves grouping millions of people together based on one common feature – skin colour, gender, religion, sexual orientation, nationality, clan or tribe – and attributing a handful of common negative characteristics to them. It is innately dehumanising because individual identity, values and character simply don't matter. Any philosophy that is premised on bigotry is a legacy of demented, irrational Europeans from centuries past. While racists fixate on skin colour, they could just as easily have chosen eye colour or nose size as anti-Semites have done with Jews for thousands of years.

Edouard Drumont, the late 19th Century, French anti-Semite described Jews as follows: "That notorious hooked nose, the blinking eyes, the clenched teeth, the jug ears, the nails cut square instead of rounded to an almond shape! The upper body is too long, Jews have flat feet, round knees, extraordinarily jutting ankles, and offer the soft, limp hand of a hypocrite and traitor. They often have one arm shorter than the other… [They have] a disagreeable aroma… which is an indication of their race and helps them recognise each other…"

It is easy to recognise the absurdity of bigotry when it is directly expressed. However, reactive anti-white racists use history to justify their stereotypes rather than direct conclusions about the innate evil of pale pigmentation. The results are just as irrational. Reactive anti-white racism pairs a Jew like me with the neo-Nazis who would like to see me exterminated; it puts the late, Jewish liberation struggle veteran Joe Slovo and neo-Nazi racist Eugene Terreblanche in the same box – all because of shared pigmentation. Anti-white bigotry reflects one of the negative legacies of colonialism – namely, a defensive refusal to address the reality that black Africans are mostly exploited, abused and killed by other black Africans. This is simply a reflection of numbers. Blacks are a majority so of course they will run governments on the continent and will suffer more at the hands of each other than at the hands of racial minorities. This does not make such suffering any more acceptable. It is of no comfort to a black African to be exploited by a fellow black African; it is of no solace to grieving relatives that at least their loved one was tortured and killed by a member of their own race and nationality.

The failure to hold black Africans accountable for crimes they commit against their own marks the primary reason why the continent lags the rest of the world, morally and economically.

It is an embarrassing disgrace that the last country on earth to outlaw slavery was Mauritania – in 2007, more than a century after most colonial powers came to their senses; to this day, 10 to 20% of Mauritania's black population remain enslaved by other blacks and anti-slavery activists are detained and tortured for their humanitarian efforts. In August 2016, 13 anti-slavery activists were sentenced to between three and 15 years imprisonment for trying to stand up for the enslaved. What sayeth the African Union? Nothing.

It took Niger until 2003 to finally declare slavery illegal – after "abolishing" it in 1960 but keeping it legal.

Eritrea is the world's third biggest source of refugees after Syria and Afghanistan primarily because of another form of slavery – indefinite national service. The Eritrean regime is so paranoid about its hostile neighbour, Ethiopia, that compulsory conscription sometimes lasts decades and constitutes endless forced labour on low pay with leave frequently denied for years. Rule breakers are held in cells or shipping containers. No wonder Eritrean men flee the continent in droves.

One of the worst post-colonial examples of the cheapness of African lives and the passivity of the continent's leaders was the 1994 Rwandan genocide. The predecessor to the AU, the Organisation of African Unity, refused to call it a genocide and the world sat by while a million Tutsis were slaughtered over the course of 100 days. Who did the OAU ultimately blame? The West – particularly France and the United States – because it was apparently their responsibility to intervene and stop the carnage! And yet when Western nations do

Photo: Martha Rial, 1997. From 'Trek of Tears', Rwanda

intervene or put human-rights or economic-policy conditions on aid, they are accused of being imperialistic and patronising.

Former US president Bill Clinton was wracked with guilt over the Rwandan genocide which he considers one of the great failures of his foreign policy; he formally apologised to the Rwandan people – but I cannot recall any African leaders expressing any guilt, taking responsibility or offering similar apologies, or even simple regret, for their inaction.

African Union solidarity is reserved for the governing elites and not for the people. This is why the organisation has proved so relentlessly useless: most African leaders are part of the problem and therefore cannot be part of the solution unless they disempower themselves and pay back the billions they have stolen. Fat chance.

The election of Nelson Mandela birthed the promise of a different attitude and foreign policy on our continent – one based on human rights rather than reflexive, unconditional defence of every African dictatorship. After all, it is contradictory to argue the obvious – that Africans have the same potential as other human beings – but then to hold them to a patronisingly lower standard of governance and human-rights observance on account of a brutal colonial past. Africa is not the only continent that has been subjected to foreign invaders and therefore we cannot keep using colonialism and racism as an excuse to explain our laggard, pathetically unequal development and lack of respect for human rights. The reality is that every inhabited continent has been a brutal mess for millennia – tribes, clans, city-states, countries and empires at war with each other – and if the root cause is perpetually diagnosed as what happened centuries ago then we are helpless to solve it.

After Mandela's short five years in office came Thabo Mbeki who ardently embraced and encouraged the elitist, defensive, unconditional unity embodied by the AU. Incredibly, he still considers his unwavering support for Robert Mugabe to be one of his biggest triumphs, despite the huge cost to the Zimbabwean people and the burden on South Africa which has had to absorb three million desperate Zimbabwean refugees into its stressed economy. Mbeki never viewed the conflict in Zimbabwe as being Mugabe versus the human rights and democratic will of the Zimbabwean people; he saw it as Africa versus the West.

Mbeki's paranoid obsession with the West spawned his outlandish views on HIV/AIDS and resistance to anti-retrovirals on account of their toxic side effects which he seemed to see as some sort of racist plot (never mind that chemotherapy and radiation therapy for cancer also have toxic side effects but are the best the medical profession can currently offer). His public health policy contributed to the deaths of 300 000 South Africans and the orphaning of more than a million children. Neither he nor the ANC has ever offered an apology to the South African people and he continues to defend his bizarre views on HIV/AIDS.

Mbeki reminds me of some Jews I know who still refuse to buy German products as though current generations of Germans are responsible for genocidal choices made before they were born. Times change. It is illegal to be a Nazi in Germany and people are imprisoned for denying the holocaust.

A scant 50 years ago, black American men couldn't vote and were being lynched by white racists; now a black man has been democratically elected president twice by a majority white electorate.

Does this mean everything is rosy in Europe and the US? Of course not. Every country is a work in progress – after all, the very concept of human rights is relatively new in broad historical terms and is constantly evolving. A century ago, human rights involved simple, obvious principles such as giving women and blacks the vote; now it encompasses acknowledging the fact that people don't choose their own sexuality any more than they choose their own skin colour.

Europeans and Americans can be hypocrites when it comes to human rights, excusing the oppression of the Palestinians, turning a blind eye to vicious human-rights abuses in the Middle East in exchange for oil, and prioritising the war against Al Shabaab and Boko Haram over human-rights concerns. However, that does not mean respect for human rights is a "Western" concept that should not matter. Surely every sane person wants "regime change" in Africa, especially in Zimbabwe whose desperate people suffer from an 80% unemployment rate?

The time for excuses is long over, the time for holding African leaders to patronisingly lower standards must end. It would take many books to describe the dreadful suffering inflicted by black Africans on each other amid despotic political leadership that creates more problems than it solves. In fact, many African leaders are not even aware of the problems suffered by their citizenry because they prohibit a free press which might enlighten them

more precisely as to the people's suffering and crushed opportunities: Whose fault is it that there is still no tarred, trans-African highway? Did European leaders lie down on the road to make sure it was never built and that Africa remained inefficient? Whose fault is it that African countries do a scant 12% of their trade with each other because it is far easier to trade with other continents than attempt to deal with each other's bureaucracies? Why do trucks have to line up at inter-African borders for days, waiting to be processed by lazy, corrupt, border bureaucrats who couldn't give a shit about the truck drivers or the economy they are trying to service? Whose fault is it that Nigeria produces crude oil but has to import refined petroleum because its four government-run refineries suffer such poor maintenance that they are perpetually incapable of operating at full capacity? Why is it acceptable for ANC politicians who make over a million rand a year to treat and pay their workers like white racists did under apartheid? How do African politicians and their children become billionaires on government salaries? Whose fault is it that Nigeria's military brass stole billions meant for military equipment to aid in the fight against Boko Haram and sent their troops into battle unprepared, knowing they were likely to die (and then charged some soldiers with treason for refusing to sacrifice themselves)? Why is it that in 80% of sub-Saharan African countries, anti-HIV drugs are available but their distribution fails at the "last mile"? The drugs make it across oceans but it is the pathetic last few kilometres to the clinics that pose the problem. Even when a country is in crisis, such as Sierra Leone during the Ebola epidemic, border bureaucrats left vital medical supplies donated by the West sitting at the airport for a month while their fellow citizens died like flies. And it took the African Union five months just to have a meeting about the Ebola outbreak – months after the West was already in full action mode.

The march from colonial liberation to self-negation and continued oppression is characterised by many complex factors for which I have no glib explanation. Why did African revolutionaries risk their lives to liberate their nations from colonialism only to continue to violate their people's human rights and steal their nations' wealth? It certainly reflects a deep-seated dehumanisation stemming from the violent patriarchy and elitism of a tradition that allows kings, chiefs and men to rule on whim – an awful foundation of cultural, economic and social oppression that was subsequently fortified by the racist contempt of colonialism. Can traditional African cultures that promote second-class status for women and unconditional respect for royals, chiefs and elders ever produce truly democratic, accountable, human-rights-based societies? Not without an ability to evolve and firmly prioritise human rights over culture and tradition.

Despite rivers of rhetoric about equality, traditional elitism in Africa, fortified by bourgeois materialism, is accepted as natural law. Traditional African cultures have one commonality: kings, chiefs, men and elders have more status and power than everyone else. Therein lies the fundamental clash between culture and a democratic society based on human rights for all: The South African government erects "speed kills" warning signs around the country but its politicians apparently believe that commonsense advisory doesn't apply to them; they speed around the country in blue-light convoys, periodically maiming

and killing citizens and it is simply considered to be a cost of doing business. Winnie Madikizela-Mandela – a member of parliament who hardly ever shows up for work – was outraged that the police dared pull her driver over for speeding. She cried racism as though it should be understood and accepted that she and all around her are exempt from the traffic laws; it was the police officers who were simply doing their jobs and had no idea she was sitting in the back seat who got suspended. Despite his profuse, frantic apologies, a Zimbabwean truck driver was recently sentenced to two years in prison and banned from driving for life for inadvertently getting in the way of the Bob and the Wailers motorcade. This is outrageous and pathetic but not unusual on our continent. African leaders and tribal royals demand obeisance and special treatment regardless of their people's interests.

Prince William drives himself around England in British-made cars with no blue lights, discreetly followed by one security vehicle, and British politicians would never be seen in expensive foreign cars blowing through traffic lights and endangering citizens. In South Africa, R15 million has been spent on imported, luxury vehicles just for President Zuma's wives. Clearly, westerners have more self-esteem and assertiveness by virtue of lengthier traditions of human rights and democracy: they value their own lives a lot more than Africans and have a far more limited tolerance for inefficiency, hypocrisy and elitism.

If black adult lives matter little in Africa, children's lives seem to matter even less – they are at the bottom of the man- woman- child hierarchy. The South Sudanese government of President Salva Kiir has begun rounding up children as young as

12 to fight in its civil war. Sixty percent of children aged five to 17 in Burkina Faso work. Children are birthed throughout the continent with scant regard for whether there are sufficient resources for them. Can there be anything more frustrating than seeing a painfully thin woman in a refugee camp pregnant with her sixth child or an unemployed man with multiple wives and a dozen children born into zero opportunity?

Workers are not just producers; they are also consumers. Lifestyle is determined by an aggregate of income, needs and prices. People can make a hundred thousand a month but if a loaf of bread costs a grand and/or they each have 10 children and two households to support, they will be relentlessly poor and beyond any macro-economic intervention. And yet it is not just politically incorrect but verboten to even mention the critical issue of poor people burdening themselves and diminishing their prospects and those of the continent by having enormous families.

Julius Malema encourages black South Africans to have as many children as possible and Jacob Zuma who has fathered over 20 children with a multitude of mothers pronounces that women are not real women until they have children.

This is insane and inhumane on so many levels: if every adult human was financially and emotionally suited to be a parent, there would be no child abandonment or neglect anywhere in the world; the reality is that every country on earth has to deal with abandoned babies and children that need to be fostered and adopted by other adults. Politicians, civic and religious leaders should be emphasising the opposite: having children is a serious emotional

commitment and financial responsibility that is best met by conscious family planning. Each child represents an expense that diminishes the resources available to the rest of the family; it is not helpful for adults, children or society for a person to have eight children unless they can afford it. These are commonsense realities that cannot be obviated by defensive, hazy references to culture or tradition. And yet trade unions want us to sympathise with a mine worker who earns R6 000 a month but chooses to have two wives and eight children, using his housing allowance for food instead of housing, and then complaining about living in a shack. Apparently, there is a macro-economic solution that will allow workers to live large no matter how many children they spawn. Well, what is it?

Across the continent, there are hideous, persecutory cultural traditions that trammel life prospects for women and children, including child marriage and female genital mutilation. Most recently, the world was introduced to the hyenas of southern Malawi, older men who are paid by parents to have sex with their daughters as soon as they experience their first menstruation.

These appalling and embarrassing facts have not stopped African leaders from continuing to point fingers at the West for the sins of the past while turning a blind eye to the present-day slavery, torture, exploitation and oppression practiced by and against their own people. The unconditional solidarity embodied by the African Union (which gets most of its budget from the West) must be discarded. How about forming an alternative organisation, consisting of a smaller group of nations that are at least theoretically committed to democracy, human rights and progress, and willing to punish dictators on the continent with economic sanctions?

Oppressive traditions and the acceptance of elitism in Africa are home-grown, self-inflicted burdens that have nothing to do with the wicked west. Until human rights are prioritised over tradition and culture, until African leaders are willing to turn away from each other on principle, Africa simply cannot progress.

Photo: 5chw4r7z

Reassessing Genocide in Africa

by Michael Schmidt

"There are no devils left in Hell. They are all in Rwanda." - a Roman Catholic priest reported in Time magazine on 16 April 1994, ten days after the Genocide began.

The Common Nature of Genocide

They came in their droves, each one in turn lighting their own tiny candle. There was the skinny young man in the brown leather jacket and cloth cap, the curvy woman in her silver-patina skirt and white blouse, the petite bald man with his severe black suit and tailored shirt, the young woman with the gold earrings matching her heels and her braids piled high on her head. Each one had lost someone in the Rwandan "Hundred Nights" Genocide of 1994 and they gathered in Johannesburg on 21 April to pay their respects to their dead – and to watch a film on the treacherous themes of forgiveness and reconciliation in atrocity-fractured societies.

The event was hosted by Constitution Hill plus the Johannesburg Holocaust and Genocide Centre, the South African History Archives, and the High Commission of Rwanda. The film screening commemorated the 22nd anniversary of the initiation of the Hundred Nights by génocidaires, and the 20th anniversary of the first Truth and Reconciliation Commission (TRC) hearing into the atrocities of the apartheid era, on 15 April 1996.

I had covered the TRC when it sat in Durban, especially the amnesty hearing of former Vlakplaas death-squad commander Dirk Coetzee, and had covered the 10th anniversary of the Hundred Nights in Kigali and Butare in 2004, so I had been invited to attend. We had an overflowing venue with perhaps 200 people, including many Rwandan Genocide and some Jewish Holocaust survivors in the audience. Before the memorial candles were lit, Rwandan High Commissioner Vincent Karenga warned about the attempt by Rwandan génocidaires – some of them sheltered by countries that had given them asylum – to reach out to "genocidal forces" abroad in the world, seeking justification for their crimes, stating that the slogan "Never Again!" would be irrelevant if education on the causes of the genocidal impulse were not vigorously pursued.

Genocide is a complex phenomenon, marred by perpetrator denialism and revisionism, but is defined by the United Nations Convention on the Prevention and Punishment of the Crime of Genocide (1948), as "any of the following acts committed with intent to destroy, in whole or in part, a national, ethnical, racial or religious group, as such: (a) Killing members of the group; (b) Causing serious bodily or mental harm to members of the group; (c) Deliberately inflicting on the group conditions of life calculated to bring about its physical destruction in whole or in part;(d) Imposing measures intended to prevent births within the group; (e) Forcibly transferring children of the group to another group."

Genocide is sadly nowhere near as rare as we'd hope – because mass scale or success are not defining factors under the Con-

To mark the closing of the mourning period commemorating the
22nd Anniversary of the genocide in Rwanda

The Johannesburg Holocaust & Genocide Centre,
and the Professional Journalists' Association of South Africa

invite you to a screening of the documentary

TELLING TRUTHS IN ARUSHA (2010)
directed by Beate Arnestad

Fifteen years after the crimes were committed,
Father Hormisdas, a Catholic priest from Rwanda,
is ready to defend himself against charges of
genocide. How does the Norwegian judge
in charge of the tribunal interpret the different
truths told by the witnesses? Unique access
to the courtroom lets us come close to the
truth behind all the lies. Truth appears to be
a relative concept. It has many faces.

The screening will be followed by a discussion

with renowned journalists

Michael Schmidt and **Hamilton 'Tony' Wende**

Date: Monday 11 July 2016

Time: 19h30

Venue: Johannesburg Holocaust & Genocide Centre, 1 Duncombe Rd (cnr Jan Smuts Ave), Forest Town

RSVP: shirley@jhbholocaust.co.za or call (011) 6403100/2148

Booking essential as seating is limited.   No charge for admission.

vention. It usually emerges within broader conditions of social collapse, such as during the implosion of failed states and the rise of the primitive accumulation of organised banditry such as in ex-Somalia, during civil war by predator states such that waged in Zaire under Mobutu Sese Seko; it is often entangled with ethnicised struggles over resources that result in pogroms as in Darfur, and sometimes with revolutionary class war in much more developed countries such as Libya during the Arab Spring.

In Africa, while sub-state actors also engage in genocide – as with the Muslim Séléka versus Christian Anti-Balaka militia in the Central Africa Republic at the moment – the privateer state is more often the perpetrator: a privateer state consists of a narrow-based consortium of hard-nosed business entrepreneurs, ethnic factional leaders adept at populist politics, a tiny bureaucratic class, and the better-trained sections of the military, usually the paratroopers (where such exist), armoured infantry and the presidential guard. The privateer state usually survives not only by extorting its citizenry, but by extending its extortionist operations into neighbouring states and often ethnicises its conflict in order to express a coherent mobilising propaganda that appeals to a distinct supranational ethnic constituency.

Is Reconciliation Desirable?

Karenga's warnings about the viability of genocidal currents in Africa today was followed by a brief set of filmed interviews with Rwandan Genocide survivors (at least two of whom I later spotted in the audience). Their stories of what happened to their families defied imagination: the one

woman spoke of her mother being turned over to the Interahamwe militia by Catholic nuns who had promised to shelter her; the génocidaires came and cut her legs off, then finding her still alive the next day, cut off her breasts, then the following day, returning to find her dying, executed her.

The documentary itself, A Snake Gives Birth to A Snake, takes its name from the chilling response of an Inkatha Freedom Party member when asked by the TRC why he had hacked a nine-month-old girl to death with a panga during the 1992 Boipatong Massacre in which 45 people were slaughtered south of Johannesburg. The film follows an ethnically diverse South African acting troupe as they recreate the roles of the most crucial interlocutors of the TRC process – that of the translators themselves – around twelve of whom are gathered together by director Michael Lessac.

With iconic musician Hugh Masekela devising songs based directly on TRC testimony ("They cut off my husband's hands..." etc), the play not only recreated the clash of competing truths at the TRC, but as the doccie shows, pitted the actors' own sense of their place in our shattered history against each other's, as they increasingly come under the strain of the burden of our political history while touring the play in Rwanda, then Northern Ireland, then ex-Yugoslavia, with veteran journalist Max du Preez documenting the process.

After each performance, the troupe gathered together audience members from all of the competing sides in the host country and held a round-table discussion on the themes raised in the play – with an especial focus on the meaning of forgiveness and whether it was desirable or possible. It was a rougher journey than either actors or film-makers had expected: in Rwanda, the point was made by one audience member that among young Rwandan school kids, the parents of half of them were murdered, and the others were in jail for genocide; in Northern Ireland, even the Catholic and Protestant dead are buried separately and one Irish National Liberation Army veteran stated that if Ireland had a TRC it would benefit the victims' families not at all because he felt no guilt for the killings he had committed; while in ex-Yugoslavia, the troupe continually ran into problems of trying to bridge the ethnic divide as it was almost impossible to secure mixed audiences, or to even screen Albanian and Serbian text translations of the play alongside each other.

At one point du Preez asked a circle of young Rwandans for advice on how to deal with the fact that with his pale skin and Afrikaans surname, he will always be presumed to be an apartheid perpetrator (in fact he was convicted of "terrorism" for his journalism), and the one young Tutsi girl responded that there were Hutus in her class and she "loved them dearly" because they allowed her to express herself from time to time in bitter outbursts against the Hutus for having initiated the Genocide; so, she said, the solution was not to run away and hide one's guilt, but to go and live among one's former victims and show them one's human face so that one day one's humanity and contrition will be accepted by them.

The film gave me serious pause for thought on my own career as a journalist: even with 26 years behind me, much of them spent working in poor black areas, I felt that I was still only part-way down a long journey of reconciliation, and the current

debate on decolonisation and the entrenched nature of cultural and structural racism underscores that many wounds are unhealed in the post-apartheid era. After the screening, I spoke informally to United Democratic Movement leader Bantu Holomisa: "Looking back at that time [Boipatong], I can't believe we made it," he said to me; "Sadly we still have much unfinished business," I replied, thinking of the 2008 Pogroms in which 62 people were slaughtered and 100,000 displaced in what was partly a genocide as defined by the Genocide Convention, and the 2012 Marikana Massacre by police of 34 striking platinum miners in what was a clear case of class war; "Yes we do," he responded.

The Tension Between Truth and Justice

Rolling forward to 11 July and the closing event of the commemoration of the Rwandan Genocide, the Holocaust and Genocide Centre screened the Beate Arnestad documentary Telling Truths in Arusha, which follows the genocide trial in Arusha, Tanzania, before the International Criminal Tribunal on Rwanda (ICTR) of Catholic priest Father Hormisdas who presided over a church and college where mass killings took place in 1994. Throughout the trial, Hormisdas sat calmly, his eyes shielded behind his spectacles, displaying no outrage at the charges, no sense of horror at the scale of the Genocide; in fact, Arnestad's camera catches him speaking privately to his defence attorney, dismissing the 800,000 death toll as nonsense.

Following the film, representing The Ulu Club for Southern African Conflict Journalists – an outfit that holds events to allow the public to interrogate journalistic ethics in covering societies in conflict – I lead a discussion on the difficult themes it raised. I stated that it perhaps helped to distinguish between veracité (fact) and verité (truth) – as the film demonstrated that fact and truth are not necessarily the same thing, neither for the survivor, nor the journalist, nor the perpetrator, nor the judicial officer presiding at Arusha, and that the search for a fact-based and fundamentally true justice is perhaps hardest of all.

It was with bitterness that I had to report, however, that the genocidal impulse was far from dead in Africa. As we met that night, forensic and eyewitness evidence was being painstakingly compiled of year-old mass graves in Angola where MPLA government forces massacred perhaps 3,000 people at Mt Sumi in April 2015, and of fresh mass graves in Mozambique as a result of the return to civil war between RENAMO and FRELIMO there.

Other recent cases of mass slaughter in Africa abound: for example, back in 2007-2008, pogroms in Kenya left perhaps 1,500 dead and perhaps 600,000 displaced. The crisis was rooted in political unrest following the contested election of President Mwai Kibaki, but opposition supporters of went on the warpath, killing members of Kibaki's' ethnic group, the Kikuyu, which immediately ethnicised the conflict, with Kikuyu striking back at the Luo and Kalejin ethnic groups.

Another example occurred in 2009 in Conakry, Guinea, when troops loyal to junta leader Captain Moussa Dadis Camara opened fire on a rally of pro-democracy activists, killing an estimated 157 people: this was merely the latest massacre by Camara's putschists who had killed 60 and 23 people respectively in general strikes held in January and February 2007, establishing martial law; the massacres reinforced the established pattern whereby Guinean privateer regimes use massacre to prop up their shaky authority against the anger of the popular classes.

The roots of the Rwandan Genocide are far more complex, but long simmering since the Belgians instituted "ethnic" classification cards in the 1950s for groups identified as Tutsis, Hutus, and Twa. But these were essentially fake ethnicities: of the 18 clans in Rwanda, all except arguably the royal clan were ethnic mixes of Nilotics,

Above: Father Hormisdas Nsengimana (right) was acquitted in 2009 of genocide as well as murder and extermination as crimes against humanity after his trial at The Hague.

Bantu and Pygmies who had intermarried over a millennium; but those classified Tutsi had to own more than 10 cattle, and it helped if they were tall; this was a class designation that had spurious racial elements appended. The result of such faux ethnicisation was 100,000 slaughtered in 1959 and 800,000 in 1994.

Structural Enablers of Hatred

One eyewitness to the Rwandan Genocide, US journalist Scott Peterson in his book Me Against My Brother (2000), came up with one of the earliest and still to my mind most viable analyses. Peterson had trawled through the looted ruins of the mansion of President Juvénal Habyarimana – the 6 April 1994 shooting down of his jet sparked the Genocide – and found there a proudly framed photograph of Tutsi homes burning during the so-called "Apocalypse Revolution" in 1959 in which 100,000 Tutsi were slaughtered, plus a book dedicated to Habyarimana by President François Mitterand, and a private Catholic chapel. These items inspired him to speculate on three structural enablers of the Genocide.

- Firstly, the deliberate cultivation of Hutu supremacist ideology, driven by Habyarimana's wife Agathe's Akazu inner circle and its extremist Zero Network of politicians and public servants, dating especially from the 1990 publication of the genocidal Hutu 10 Commandments by the extremist newspaper Kangura! (Awake!), then the formation by Habyarimana of the ruling MRND party's Interahamwe militia, and the state's Coalition por la Défense de la République (CDR) and its Impuzamugambe militia, and then – and this is often forgotten – the "trial runs" of massacre that had already left around 2,000 people dead in the two years before the Genocide began.

- Secondly, the unblanching support by France for the MRND regime, regardless of its growing extremism – including the uninterrupted supply of weapons shipments even during the height of the Genocide when the extent of the killings was obvious. The French flew Agathe Habyarimana and select Akazu members to safety in Paris just after the Genocide began, and Mitterand officially welcomed at the Quay d'Orsay at the end of April 1994 – during the Genocide – Hutu extremist Foreign Minister Jérôme Bicamumpaka (acquitted by the Arusha Tribunal in 2011) and CDR commander and hate radio head Jean-Bosco Barayagwiza (later convicted of genocide; died in 2010).

- Lastly (and this touched on the theme of the film), the acquiescence of the Catholic Church as the preparations for genocide became irreversible, especially because since Belgian missionaries had supported the 1959 Genocide, following independence in 1962, the Church had become so integrated into the Hutu regime that the Archbishops of Kigali, including the incumbent during the Genocide, Vincent Nsengiyumva (who was killed as a perpetrator by the RPF), were invariably high MRND leaders as well, and in some cases such as at the Ste Famille Cathedral in Kigali, during the Genocide, priests such as Father Wenceslas Munyeshyaka openly wore pistols, expressed Hutu supremacist views and allowed the death-squads to select from among those seeking sanctuary there for killing (he was later convicted of genocide at Arusha but continues to live freely in France).

Widening Circles of Ethnicised Conflict

At the commemoration event, I introduced Hamilton Wende, a South African journalist who worked as the sound-man on a BBC crew that went to Rwanda during the Genocide with the almost impossible mission objective of trying to explain why the Genocide was happening. In his book True North (1995), as with Peterson, Wende also spoke of the impact of Belgian ethnic classification in the 1950s and Belgian support for the 1959 Genocide, but unlike Peterson's work which had the benefit of six years of hindsight, Tony's work is marked by the immediacy of being plunged deep into the moral twilight zone of the Genocide as it was unfolding.

He used some resonant phrases such as "spiral of madness" to describe what he was seeing – but the one that may assist us here is "Republic of Dementia," and he described his journey into what he called an "incoherence of darkness," "half-drowning in a spiritual Interzone, grasping at the flimsy edges of our own rationality," as both a physical and metaphysical journey.

And as Karenga warned, the perpetrators' revisionism was already attempting to establish its legitimacy: back in 1994 we see Wende interview the mayor of the nearest town in the Nyarubuye Parish where some 4,000 people were slaughtered by the génocidaires: the interview takes place in the UN's Bonacco refugee camp, full of tens of thousands of perpetrators, and as Hutu extremist radio pushes out a revisionist line over the airwaves of the refugee camp, claiming it is the Tutsi "invading cockroaches" who are committing genocide, the mayor, who is accused of organising the Nyarubuye massacre, reveals his true self by evoking nasty anti-Tutsi sentiments.

The Rwandan nightmare, in which the génocidaires hacked their names into our hearts with spiked clubs and machetes, is properly condemned – but its memory has also been used by the post-Genocide regime to prop up its despotic authority, and to justify punitive raids into neighbouring countries, transforming contemporary Rwanda into a privateer state and generating ever widening circles of instability, ethnic and ethnicised conflict in the Great Lakes region. Rwanda is not the last we have seen of genocide.

Preventing Pogroms

But I want to end on a more hopeful note – because genocide is not inevitable. Ideally, the preconditions for genocide should be recognised by adequate early-warning systems that monitor génocidaire revisionist activities and that can motivate the international community to prevent or curtail the construction of institutional systems that facilitate mass killings. Community resistance is also vital as demonstrated during the 2008 Pogroms in South Africa: comparing Alexandra Section 2, east of Johannesburg, known as "Beirut" and Section 5, known as "Setswala," Jean-Pierre Misago of Wits University's Forced Migration Studies Programme, co-author of a the report for the International Organisation for Migration (IOM) on the Pogroms, said Beirut had succumbed to the killings while Setswala had fended off attempts by the pogromists to spark killings in their neighbourhood.

"The Section 5 community comrades met the Section 2 pogromists at the border of Section and told them 'no, you can't come in here; we will sort out our own foreigners, because you don't know who they are'." You can bet the Setswala reception committee was armed to the teeth, to back up their ploy, but it worked, keeping the killers at bay while Setswala's foreigners were helped to leave town quickly, their vigilant neighbours keeping watch over their homes to ensure no-one looted them. Critical to their success was that there was no institutional support for the killings as there had been in Rwanda, but the lesson was clear: when communities stood together, they managed to prevent the pogroms from spreading.

However, I argued in the wake of the Pogroms that community defence must go beyond mere moral encouragement: it must firstly be strongly armed, with legal firearms not just knives and clubs, to meet force with force; secondly it must prepare in advance safe zones that operated like Setswala in Alexandra, where those in danger are sheltered and where pogromists fear to tread; and thirdly, it must establish local networks like the street committees of the anti-apartheid struggle to gather intelligence and co-ordinate actions. Today I would add that such networks must act as bellwethers for the likes of Amnesty International but also for new continental organisations such as the Pan-African Human Rights Defenders Network (PAHRDN) to enable a vigorous multilateral intervention that compels authorities in the afflicted state to suppress the genocidal impulse, dismantle its operational organs, and actively undermine the viability of the virus of the genocidal idea by combating hate speech and revisionism at all levels of society.

Michael Schmidt is a veteran investigative journalist, researcher, journalism trainer, free press activist, and published non-fiction author based in Johannesburg. He is the administrative secretary of the Professional Journalists' Association of South Africa (ProJourn) and manages its projects. The Ulu Club for Southern African Conflict Journalists, and the Southern African Cities of Refuge Project which aims to get regional cities on board the International Cities of Refuge Network (ICORN) www.icorn.org, providing safe haven for persecuted journalists, writers, musicians, and visual artists.

A Year Of Elections
(and some democracy...)

2016 has been a busy year for elections. While much of the world focuses attention on the drama playing out in America's general election, where the most qualified person to ever run for the highest office in arguably the world, goes toe-to-toe with the least qualified ever to run for perhaps any office, save the one in his own ivory (ersatz gold?) tower, the continent, meanwhile, faces local and general elections in 27 countries.

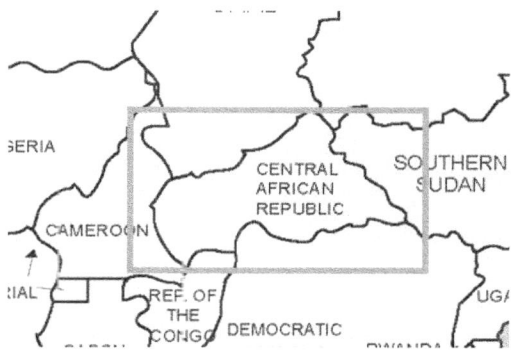

CENTRAL AFRICAN REPUBLIC:

The CAR swore in its new President in February, the first elected leader of the country since rebels ousted the last government three years ago. The French had waded in to its former colony after Muslim fighters seized power in 2013 and who then stepped aside under international pressure when they were accused of committing atrocities against Christian civilians. The wave of violence across the north send around 30,000, around two-thirds of whom are unaccompanied children, searching for safe shelter in Chad and Cameroon - countries already struggling to find resources for their own people. As if July wasn't bad enough, August saw a breakout of cholera, where at least 66 people are said to be infected. With accessibility almost impossible, and a lack of clean water, UNICEF and other agencies are straining to do what it can to help.

NIGER:

In the face of attacks from Boko Haram, security and alleviating poverty were top issues in the February/March elections. The incumbent lacked the majority in the first round of voting, but since the opposition boycotted the second round, President Mahamadou Issoufou retains his seat with a significant majority.

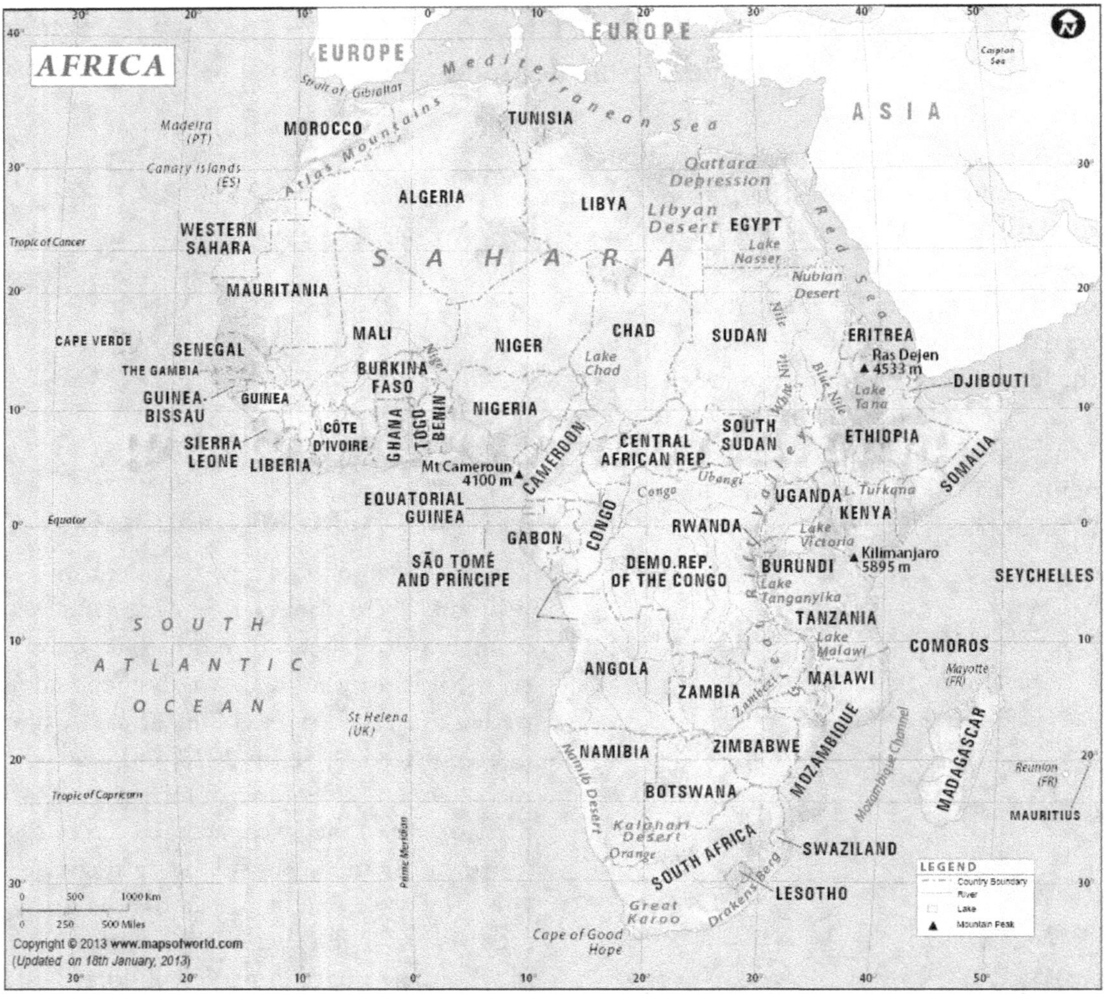

AFRICA

Map labels: EUROPE, EUROPE, Caspian Sea, ASIA, Strait of Gibraltar, Mediterranean Sea, Madeira (PT), MOROCCO, TUNISIA, Atlas Mountains, Qattara Depression, Canary Islands (ES), ALGERIA, LIBYA, Libyan Desert, EGYPT, Red Sea, Lake Nasser, WESTERN SAHARA, SAHARA, Nubian Desert, Tropic of Cancer, MAURITANIA, White Nile, CAPE VERDE, MALI, NIGER, CHAD, SUDAN, ERITREA, Ras Dejen ▲ 4533 m, SENEGAL, THE GAMBIA, BURKINA FASO, Lake Chad, Black Nile, Lake Tana, DJIBOUTI, GUINEA-BISSAU, GUINEA, NIGERIA, BENIN, TOGO, GHANA, CÔTE D'IVOIRE, CAMEROON, SOUTH SUDAN, CENTRAL AFRICAN REP., ETHIOPIA, SIERRA LEONE, LIBERIA, Mt Cameroun 4100 m, SOMALIA, Equator, EQUATORIAL GUINEA, Congo, Ubangi, UGANDA, KENYA, L. Turkana, GABON, CONGO, RWANDA, Lake Victoria, DEMO. REP. OF THE CONGO, Kilimanjaro ▲ 5895 m, BURUNDI, SÃO TOMÉ AND PRÍNCIPE, Lake Tanganyika, SEYCHELLES, TANZANIA, Lake Malawi, COMOROS, SOUTH ATLANTIC OCEAN, ANGOLA, ZAMBIA, MALAWI, Mayotte (FR), St Helena (UK), Zambezi, MOZAMBIQUE, MADAGASCAR, Reunion (FR), Tropic of Capricorn, NAMIBIA, ZIMBABWE, MAURITIUS, Namib Desert, Mozambique Channel, Prime Meridian, BOTSWANA, Kalahari Desert, Orange, Drakensberg, SWAZILAND, SOUTH AFRICA, Great Karoo, LESOTHO, Cape of Good Hope

LEGEND — Country Boundary, River, Lake, ▲ Mountain Peak

Copyright © 2013 www.mapsofworld.com
(Updated on 18th January, 2013)

Map labels: SOUTHERN SUDAN, ETHIOPIA, UGANDA, KENYA, RWANDA, Lake Victoria, BURUNDI

UGANDA:

Uganda's general election was held in February, and amidst claims of election fraud and intimidation, Yoweri Museveni was re-elected to the office he has held since 1986. Inclement weather was to blame for the 3-hour delay in getting the ballot papers flown in from South Africa, but that didn't stop conspiracy theories from flowing.

COMOROS:

The leader of the 1999 coup is once more in the top seat, having stepped down from office in 2006 when his first term ended. The results were disputed by the loser, but Azali Assoumani has been sworn into office. The complicated relationship with former colonizer, France, leaving the island of Mayotte as a French department (a move declared illegal by the United Nations), causes conflict and division as Mayotte receives excellent benefits of its situation, including full healthcare, education, and welfare services, leaving the other three islands to struggle against persistent poverty.

Constitutionally, the presidency is supposed to rotate every four years between the country's three islands, Grande Comore, Anjouan and Mohéli.

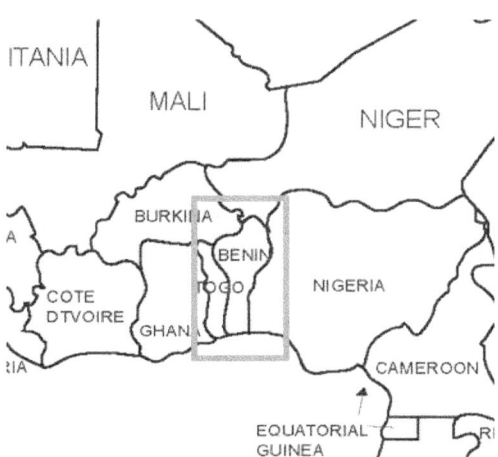

BENIN:

The Presidential election was originally postponed from 28 Feb until 6 March (the second round followed on 20 March). The result was businessman, Patrice Talon, aka "The King of Cotton" for his involvement in the cotton industry, is now Benin's 5th elected president since the Republic was formed as a multi-party system in 1960.

CAPE VERDE:

With a Parliamentary as well as a Presidential election in March 2016, and a higher than 65% voter turnout, Cape Verde saw the ousting of the ruling party after 15 years, and a decisive win for the opposition. The Presidential elections take place in October.

SENEGAL:

Senegal saw a constitutional referendum in March 2016, with changes including shortening the presidential term from 7 to 5 years, expanded authority to local authorities, some changes to land ownership, among other options to strengthen the democracy. However, with 250 registered political parties, many of which do not run candidates in elections, time will tell in the 2017 and 2019 elections, if these changes have impacted anything of substance.

ZANZIBAR (AUTONOMOUS REGION WITHIN TANZANIA):

In March 2016, the Government of National Unity in the semi-independent archipelago, faced having to form another coalition government. According to their Constitution, the President (who won over 91% of the vote) is required to select a First Vice-President from the opposition party which wins at least 10% of the votes. Unfortunately, the closest opposition party in this election only received 3%, but in a peaceful bending of the rules party leader, Seif Sharif Hamad, was appointed to the position.

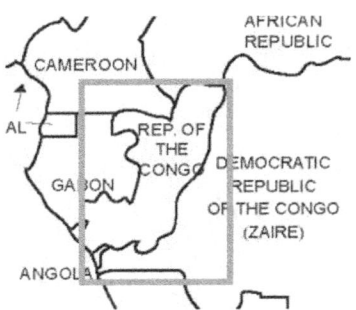

REPUBLIC OF THE CONGO:

Presidential elections held under the new constitution resulted in the formerly limited to two term president, Denis Sassou Nguesso, being allowed to run for a third term – which he won with 67% of the vote. His opposition, who won nearly 17% of the vote, announced they would rather recognize their own set of results, which it claimed was more accurate. After weeks of drama, Nguesso was sworn in as President in April.

DJIBOUTI:

Speaking of multiple terms, President Ismail Omar Guelleh was elected to a fourth term in April 2016, which at 68 makes him still within the legal age limit for presidents of Djibouti, being a maximum of 75 years old. Djibouti is on the lower ranks of press freedom, and the governing party is known to expel journalists, as well as curb freedom of assembly, to retain their tight grip on power.

BURKINA FASO:

Municipal elections – always truly the most important elections as local governance has the most direct impact on the people, and it's also where those who rise to national office learn the ropes of governance – were held in Burkina Faso in August. For the first time, cellphone apps played a role in ensuring a free and fair election with Burkina Open Data Initiative (Bodi) creating the Open Election app cutting the time results were known from 2 weeks down to a matter of hours. With results being readily available on an open web portal, media, advocacy groups, and election observers had access to analyze the results almost immediately.

SAO TOME & PRINCIPE:

With the first round of voting annulled, the second round boycotted by the incumbent President Manual Pinto da Costa, Sao Tome and Principe now have a new President, Evaristo Carvalho.

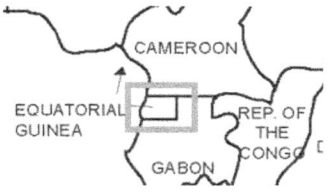

EQUATORIAL GUINEA:

Bringing the date of an election forward 7 months, receiving nearly 94% of the vote, shutting down Human Rights Watch days before the election, beating up opposition members, incumbent President Teodoro Obiang Nguema Mbasogo remains president for a second term. According to their constitution, he is allowed two terms of 7 years, although he has been in office since 1979, after he ousted his uncle in a bloody coup. Equatorial Guinea is said to the richest country per capita in Africa and has one of the worst human rights records in the world.

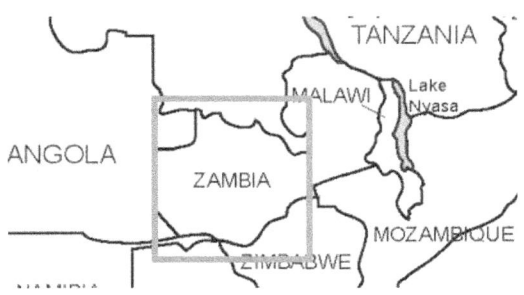

ZAMBIA:

A hard fought election in Zambia saw incumbent President Edgar Lungu retaining his office and opposition parties accusing the Electoral Commission of Zambia of colluding with the winning party – those accusations appear to be supported by independent observers, including the European Union, and this may end up in court before long.

SOUTH AFRICA:

South Africa's elections always receive international scrutiny, and 2016 was no different. A hard fought battle, largely between the incumbent majority party, the ANC led by the diminishing stature of Jacob Zuma, and the Democratic Alliance (DA) had everyone in a tizzy. It has long been believed that the ANC would hold onto power for about as long as the old National Party had, but with a free press comes an often uncomfortable spotlight, and constant reports of ANC leaders' corruption and cronyism, has left many voters with a bad taste in the mouth. As a result, the DA appeared to surprise even themselves as they made huge gains, even in traditionally ANC areas. Coalition talks for control of the economic capital of the country, Johannesburg, are ongoing.

SEYCHELLES:

It is a paradise, a peaceful and idyllic island life with a reputation for protecting celebrities like the Alamuddin -Clooneys on their honeymoon. Nobody knows the names of the 193 voters who ensured President James Michel's re-election. That small a number, in a population of 90,000 people, sees the Supreme Court scrutinizing the results.

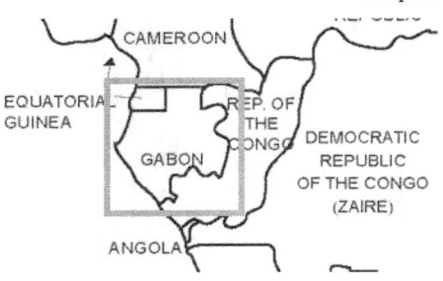

GABON:

August saw the Gabonese heading to the polls amidst a host of candidates, some campaigning on constitutional reform, and few surprises to a change at the top were expected. The Gabonese Democratic Party has held power since independence from France in 1960.

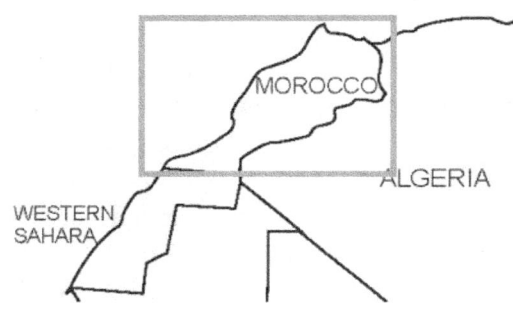

MOROCCO:

With its multi-party system, and little chance of one party gaining full power, a coalition government is the expected order of the day come October 2016. The "forgotten conflict", assuredly forgotten by everyone expect Sahrawis demanding their right to self-determination in Western Sahara, remains a note of contention.

SOMALIA:

September and October see parliamentary elections in Somalia – the first "truly free" elections since 1969 (according to the President). Another complicated system exists here: suffrage is limited with only 13,750 voters out of a population of 10,5 million. 135 tribal clan elders hold significant authority in their respective clans and while the lower house exists, the upper house of Parliament is yet to be established. To add to the complexities of establishing a basic administrative system, the militant group, Al-Shabab continues to rampage through the country, with car bombings and suicide attacks on mostly government officials and buildings occurring almost daily.

THE GAMBIA:

Crackdowns and oppression against freedom of expression and assembly seem to be the order of the day in the months leading up to elections in December. Reports of opposition members being beaten with hose pipes and batons have not been confirmed, but the country's history makes the reports unsurprising.

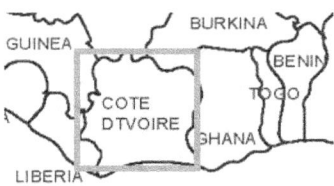

IVORY COAST:

Parliamentary elections will be held in December 2016, following the presidential elections of 2015, which were a landslide victory (84%) for President Alassane Ouattara, who has been credited with managing the country well after the war. Ouattara comes from a long line of Muslim African rulers, and is married to a French business-woman who converted from Judaism to Catholicism in a ceremony presided over by former French President Sarkozy.

GHANA:

Scheduled for December 2016, Ghana seems to be following its reputation for democratic governance, and at this point, there is no certainty as to which party will win. One way the current governing party is trying to win is to make some heavy investments in infrastructure, improving roads, hospitals, and schools.

DEMOCRATIC REPUBLIC OF CONGO:

With reports that opposition to President Kabila extending his constitutionally-mandated term limit to a third term has been dealt with in a "brutal crackdown", and activists from Human Rights Watch denied access, the chances of the DRC elections being held before the end of the year, remains in doubt.

LIBYA:

It's complicated.

It's not the nature of this Editorial staff to make such an easy cop-out, but it really would be necessary to write several pages simply to summarize Libya at this point.

Paradise Undermined

The third of a four-part sampling from John GI Clarke's writing on the raging development conflict on the Pondoland Wild Coast, in the Eastern Cape province of South Africa.

by John GI Clarke

Jubaeopsis caffra, the Tree of Life

This instalment is an edited version of a chapter from John's book *The Promise of Justice. Book One: History*, published by Brevitas Publishers and available from www.thewildcoaster.co.za, It relates how the media cordon erected by the Qunya brothers was broken by a TV crew from the SABC environmental program 50/50, in October 2006. That was ten years ago. In the light of what has happened since, the chapter is full of exquisite irony.

The story so far…

Sinegugu 'Nkomba' Zukulu and I have teamed up to "Name, Unmask and Engage the Powers" who lie behind a dune mining scheme to 'tame' the magnificent

Wild Coast. Not only is a unique Tree of Life – Jubaeopsis Caffra – the Nkomba Palm, threatened by the mining ambitions of Australian mining entrepreneur, Mark Caruso, but the last traces of a very ancient pre-historic tribe of hominid's from the Sangoan-era could disappear if the mining goes ahead. That is because ancient stone age tools lie buried in the same dunes that contain rich deposits of heavy minerals.

Caruso has successfully recruited local strongman, Zamile Qunya and his younger brother Zamokwake 'Bashin' Qunya to serve his mining and money-making ambitions. The Qunya brothers lose the first round of confrontation.

The death threats start.

The Animal in the Earth

'We haven't had this much rain ever in Pondoland before. Why is this, people are asking. People have noticed that it is since the mining company has come to the area that all this rain has come, which is now too much for us. People are saying that it is because the mining company is disturbing the earth, the animal inside the earth has been upset, and is sending all this rain. My people believe, and I believe too, that all this rain is falling because the earth animal is angry with the disturbance of the earth by the mining company.'

George Cilo, Community Induna.

This explanation of abnormal climatic conditions was offered by a wise old Induna, Mr George Cilo, during a meeting of community leaders who had gathered to express their concerns to a television film crew from the SABC environmental programme – 50/50*. Representatives from all significant sectors (health, churches, traditional authorities, ANC youth, ANC veterans, business, etc.) were huddled in the Baleni Senior Secondary School library, hoping at last to have their grievances, complaints and frustrations broadcast to a wider audience, beyond the rutted roads and muddy dongas (ditches) that isolated them from civil services and support.

Baleni's proud son, Sinegugu 'Nkomba' Zukulu and I, had arranged for the crew to see for themselves the difficulties constraining learners and teachers at his alma mater.

Besides Mr Cilo's fearful subterranean beast, other more tangible animals expressed interest in our visit. Several horses were grazing in the school grounds, having carried some riders (including the head-master who had to leave his car parked some distance away) to the meeting. They were the only feasible means of transport, given the appalling condition of the roads. The moment that our interpreter translated the Induna's comment, the headmaster's horse gave vent to a loud whinny, as if to endorse this diagnosis of the bad state of affairs.

For all his apparent lack of scientific precision, the Induna's conviction lent authenticity to the meeting. This was not a pre-rehearsed media conference to lobby public sympathy; this was an opportunity for a new consciousness to emerge.

The Induna's intuitive discernment of the connection between human interference with the earth and abnormal precipitation from the heavens animated two rivers of thought, flowing in opposite yet complementary directions, making their way to the same ocean. Think Globally: Act Locally – the mantra of all environmentalists – bubbled up from its sleep in my head, stirred to life by the idea of an animal in the earth. I sat behind the scene, observing the interaction between people and the camera as it panned around the room, capturing images that would bring 50/50 viewers into the Baleni Senior Secondary School library – without the inconvenience of having to drive the challenging 4x4 obstacle course, or having to seek help from a horse.

When Sandra, the producer, was satisfied that she had enough footage for the 50/50 report and had put her technological beast back in its cage, I asked the group if I could address them, so that Nkomba and I could clarify our interest and purpose in bringing the TV crew to Baleni.

Here is an edited version of what 'the ani-

Photo courtesy: John GI Clarke

mal in the earth' prompted me to say:

'Five years ago my family (i.e. in 2001 as this was written in 2006) and I found ourselves enjoying, for the first time in our lives, the cultural richness of the Mpondo people and the scenic splendour of the Wild Coast. We were there as eco-tourists, riding a four-day horse trail with Amadiba Adventures. The memorable experience had a significant impact on our family life, not only because of the memories we cherish of that experience, but because it introduced us to the joys of horse riding and a love of horses. We returned nine months later with another family, close friends, who were eager to experience the same excitement we had enjoyed.

Our trail leader and guide was a young man named Mzamo Dlamini. He taught us something about horses that has become a parable for understanding what we mean when we talk about humans having a 'sustainable relationship' with the natural world.

On our return from a wonderfully happy time at Mtentu Estuary, my friend challenged me to a horse race across an open stretch of beach. We spurred our mounts into a gallop to see who would reach an outcrop of rocks about 500 metres away. Our trusting horses obediently complied and before we knew it we were at the rocks, narrowly avoiding riding headlong into them. I think I won, but it wasn't a happy victory, because, when Mzamo and the rest of the group caught up with us, the permanent smile on his face was gone. He took us aside and scolded us for our recklessness:

"Don't you know that horses cannot see straight ahead of themselves?" he asked, angrily. "You could have injured them - and yourselves."

He explained the eyes of a horse are positioned on either side of their heads so they can watch for predators while grazing. This gives them the ability to see both left and right, but there is an approximately 35 degree angle 'blind spot' ahead of them. "Horses trust the human on their back for forward vision. A horse will obediently ride straight over a cliff if that is where the rider directs it."

Photo courtesy: John GI Clarke

I thanked the community for producing a young man of such wisdom and went on to explain my motives in coming back to Pondoland.

'When the headmaster's horse applauded the Induna's comments earlier, it reminded me of Mzamo's teaching. But I think there is a deeper lesson we need to learn. A horse and a human rider together have four eyes. As a unit they can see almost all around. The only blind spot is an angle of about 30 degrees behind the horse, at the rider's back.

My deep fear is that the people interested in mining at Xolobeni are coming to ride on the back of the Amadiba community, and that the direction they are steering you toward is dangerous. As a social worker I am expected to challenge injustice and exploitation, and to seek always the best interests of the most vulnerable members of society. My work is to ensure access to information and services, and to promote understanding and insight about the social problems people experience. Looking back, it seems to me that wherever there is much money to be made, especially from mining operations and large construction projects, those people who stand to make the most money don't really care what happens to vulnerable people living on the land, or to the environment – the earth, water, plants and animals – in the long term.

Sinegugu asked me to bring the TV cameras to see the hardship you have to bear. From what I have seen and heard, I am now excited again that the wonderful blessings that my family and I experienced five years ago can be experienced by other people. I told many people about the Amadiba Adventures horse trail, and they also came to spend money in this area.

I live in Johannesburg, and work closely with friends in Soweto to bring foreign tourists to visit Soweto. I believe those same tourists would love also to come to the Wild Coast and spend money here.

When I return again, if you wish me to, I would like to bring with me more of my friends to learn from the wisdom of the Mpondo people, to learn from people like Mzamo and the Induna.'

Circumstances then conspired to separate me from the TV crew.

I had underestimated my fuel needs because the appalling road conditions had compelled me to engage four-wheel-drive most of the way. The nearest filling station was two hours away. But the kindly headmaster, Mr Nkululeko 'Pitso' Msabane, had a reserve of some diesel fuel with which to help me. To spare his horse the burden of having to carry him back to his car, I gave Mr Msabane a lift and then followed him to his homestead. Then I realised that I had no cash on me. 'No problem,' he said. I could pay him later when I had money. Besides the 20 litres of diesel added to my tank, he threw in four sticks of sugar cane as a gift, and went off on other business. I was left alone to contemplate the dramatic experiences of the morning.

While I waited in the peaceful rural setting for the TV crew to meet up with me, I tried to organise my jumbled thoughts and emotions – to 'fast and pray'. The fast was involuntary as my lunch pack was in the other vehicle, and one can eat only so much sugar cane, but the prayer was intentional. I was feeling intellectually troubled, physically scared and emotionally anxious – always good incentives for prayer, even for those not habitually given to praying.

I was troubled because, despite the apparent superstition inherent in the Induna's warning, it was in its own way strangely prophetic. He may well have been mistaken in connecting the local events of 'mining' and 'rainfall' too directly, and yes, he may have used the language of religion and myth rather than a scientific vocabulary, but the essential truth of what he was saying could not be denied. It is the same 'inconvenient truth' that Al Gore was trying to tell the world. The extreme weather events, which the elderly Induna had said were unparalleled in his lifetime were due to global warming.

Global warming happens because the earth's natural carbon cycle has been abnormally accelerated and intensified by carbon emissions from fuel derived from fossils (veritable 'animals in the earth') extracted from the earth's crust. Left to run its natural course, the carbon cycle normally takes millions of years to revolve, since it involves subduction of organic matter by the complex dynamics of tectonic plate movements in the earth's crust. Human energy demands have accelerated this process to what amounts to nano-seconds in geological time. Sustainable use of fossil fuels means that we should use them at a rate equivalent to their creation by the earth's geological systems. I started wondering how long nature had taken to create the 20 litres of fossil fuel that Mr Msabane had generously provided for me. How much had it really cost nature to produce these 20 litres? How much will our children have to pay for our extravagance? These were the thoughts that troubled me.

I was scared because I wondered if I had overstepped the mark with my impulsive speech earlier, and was courting reprisals from those who had already sold out to the ambitions of the mining company. But my fear was more a matter of fearing that the local residents would fear me. After all, who was I to judge them if they had accepted the enticements of already rich people bearing expensive gifts, if this promised some relief from the hardships they had to endure? Moral responsibility ultimately rested with those remote interests who really couldn't care less about what happened to local people or the environment, so long as they could get their fix. Even so, my social worker training had taught me to promote insights which can emerge only if one takes a non-judgemental approach to people with addictions and dependencies, whether to alcohol and drugs or to fossil fuels and heavy minerals like titanium [note this was written before the release of the film Avatar, which ironically portrays exactly that addiction – the dependency of earthlings on a rare gravity defying mineral 'unobtanium' found only on a distant planet Pandora].

I was anxious because I was beginning to doubt that I could match my walk to my talk. On the spur of the moment I had raised expectations. What possible influence can a 'stale, pale, male' have, desperately trying to extend his shelf life in the new South Africa?

Moreover, although social workers are professionally obliged to intervene to help vulnerable members of communities, the dividing line between intervention and interference is as ambiguous as the line between activism and advocacy – it all depends who is drawing it. Certain powers were not going to like what I had said, and they had deep pockets with which to fight legal battles. I had nothing but my mixed reputation and professional indemnity insurance to rely on, if they deemed it worthwhile to charge me for unprofessional conduct. Anglo Platinum had tried, unsuccessfully as it happens, to rob Richard Spoor of his professional mandate as an attorney, simply because he tried to hold them accountable to rural communities who were blessed – or cursed – with valuable minerals under their land and villages.

Eventually the camera crew arrived, breaking my fast and bringing answers to at least the prayer to "give us this day our daily bread".

Mr Zamile Qunya, Chairman of the Amadiba Coastal Community Development Association (ACCODA) Trust, which stood accused of betraying the community's trust, had called to say he would consider granting an interview, provided the community leaders gave him a mandate. We were to report to the Umgungundlovu Komkhulu the next day. The Komkhulu (Great Place) has a community hall, which had been built from the proceeds of the Amadiba Adventures eco-tourism enterprise.

Photo courtesy: John GI Clarke

Before the sun rose over the beautiful Mtentu estuary, we hastily packed up and headed for the venue. Mr Qunya greeted us courteously but asked that we wait outside while he consulted with the gathering of community leaders about obtaining their mandate. While we waited I noticed two women tilling the soil in the field below. Behind them a red umbrella shaded a bundle of blankets. Separating from the TV crew, Sinegugu and I approached the

women and asked if they would mind having their photo taken. They happily agreed and posed, smiling broadly.

'Nkosikasi, am I correct in thinking that you have a baby sleeping under that red umbrella?' I asked.

The smile grew even broader. 'Yes, Numsane, that is my baby girl. She is now three weeks old.'

Proudly she unwrapped the bundle to

Photo courtesy: John GI Clarke

show us her baby, sleeping peacefully in the field that her mother was busy tilling, so that maize could be planted and harvested when she was old enough to be weaned. A three-week-old infant, born into this spectacular rural setting, sleeping peacefully in the tilled field, beautiful and unaware of the history she will inherit.

What history: will she know the truth? Will Mr Msabane and Baleni Senior Secondary School be able to serve her as it served Sinegugu? Will she be allowed to tell us her own truth? A truth perhaps whispered to her by the 'animal in the earth' as she lay sleeping in a tilled furrow.

We returned to the TV crew to find Sandra and Richard in some consternation. Mr Qunya claimed that the gathering of men had unanimously decided that 'since we had not got their permission to talk to people in the community, they refused to grant us an interview with him'. They had been told they were not welcome and had been advised to leave.

So we left, spurred on by Sinegugu who became anxious when he noticed a notorious taxi operator and warlord driving nearby.

STOP PRESS: *In the midst of finalizing the above instalment for re-publication, MRC announced to its shareholders on 18th July 2016 that the board of directors had come to a decision to disinvest from the Xolobeni mineral sands project, and would be selling its 56% shareholding to an obscure private company known as Keysha Investments Pty Ltd.*

Was Mark Caruso finally 'dismounting' the Amadiba 'horse'?

Perhaps, but not before an attempt to flog it one last time.

The day after his announcement, on 19th July I was served with a high court summons from him, citing seven instances in which he alleges that I have defamed him and MRC. He is suing me for a combined total of R2.25 million.

Had Mr Caruso stopped there maybe I would have felt a bit rattled and defensive. But he did not. A short while later my 'horse riding instructor' Mzamo Dlamini got served with papers claiming R2 million for defamation, because of statements Mzamo had made in a live radio interview on a talk show hosted by Redi Tlhabi on Capetalk and Radio 702. See http://www.capetalk.co.za/articles/12677/resource-rich-xolobeni-eyed-by-australian-company-for-mining-exploits,

As if that was not enough 'skin in the game' obligingly Mr Caruso went even further and served summons on Cormac Cullinan, our attorney, for another R1 million for damages because of things Cormac had said in the program about outside interests causing conflict within the community and MRC misrepresenting local support for the mining. Had Mr Caruso googled Cormac's name he would have seen that he is a world renowned environmental attorney and was named among an international fellowship of "Planet Savers" in a 2008 book profiling "301 extraordinary environmentalists".

I hope readers are looking forward to reading the final instalment as much as I am looking forward to writing it.

* The 20 minute documentary, produced by Sandra Herrington for 50/50 can be viewed at this link. https://youtu.be/ux-8ryyWCT-A. Filming was done in October 2006, and the program titled "Wild Coast Corruption: Paradise Lost" was broadcast in December 2006.

Photo: Cheryl Alexander

Statement from Val Payn of Sustaining The Wild Coast, an organization dedicated to long-term sustainability of livelihoods of people who depend on the Wild Coast region:

Sikhosiphi 'Bazooka' Rhadebe. from Mdatya village in Amadiba, was gunned down outside at his home in Lurholweni township on the evening of Tues 22 March, which ironically was one day after South Africans celebrated Human Rights day. Rhadebe was Chairman of the local community activist group, the Amadiba Crisis Committee (ACC) which has fiercely but peacefully resisted proposed plans by the Australian mining group Mineral Commodities Ltd (MCR) and their local subsidiaries Transworld Energy and Mineral Resources (TEM) and local partner Xolobeni Empowerment Company (Xolco) to strip mine for mineral sands in the area. Anti-mining activists firmly believe that mining in the area will destroy their homeland, their traditional way of life, and their communities.

The assassination follows many years of continual harassment and intimidation of anti-mining activists in the area.

South African civil society has widely condemned the murder as an attack on democracy itself, and is calling on the international community, human rights organizations and civil society to petition the South African government to immediately stop its support for the mining proposal.

More details can be found on the website www.swc.org.za

That which causes conflict you may not call "development" - Sinegugu 'Nkomba' Zukulu

Photo: Cheryl Alexander

The author at Xolobeni

The Continued Rape of Africa

By Leigh Barrett

Lest one think that the drama unfolding with Xolobeni on the East coast of South Africa was all that Perth-based company, Mineral Commodities Ltd ("MRC") is doing, fear not. There's more.

Approximately 400 kms north of Cape Town on the largely uninhabited by humans pristine beaches of the west coast, MRC's local branch, Tormin, continues the pillaging of the country's natural minerals. The beaches at Matzikama Municipality, host some of the richest concentrated grades of naturally occurring zircon, ilmenite, rutile and garnet, delivering yields of around 1.6 million tonnes in 2015 alone, according to the MRC quarterly report and website.

After a catastrophic cliff collapsed in December 2015 – a feature that appears to be missing in their quarterly report of that period, the Mail & Guardian newspaper reported at the time:

"Among other breaches, Tormin is accused of expanding the mine without authorisation under the National Environmental Management Act; mining garnet in violation of the environmental management plan; mining in conservation areas; using unauthorised roads to transport products; and pumping raw sewage into the sea.... It is also accused of causing the collapse of the beachfront cliff below its processing plant through inefficient control of the plant and operating too close to the cliff in breach of approval conditions." (*http://mg.co. za/article/2015-12-14-00-state-accused-of-letting-torm-in-damage-west-coast*)

Environmentalists continue to report a lack of controls at the plant, resulting in extensive damage to vegetation, causing erosion to the sensitive cliffs and beaches.

They report that, despite being told by officials at the Department of Mineral Resources (DMR) that when Tormin was told to conduct an environmental assessment, the company simply went higher up the food chain to get the application pushed through.

(This mirrors past allegations against Executive Chairman of MRC, Mark Caruso who, in his previous position as head of Allied Gold Mining PLC, was at the center of a corruption scandal in the Solomon Islands in 2014, when he paid for a top official's children to go to an exclusive boarding school in exchange for greasing the wheels on a gold mining permit. He resigned his position to take over management of MRC.)

Strike action by the National Union of Mineworkers began with NUM members presenting a memorandum to the DMR's offices in Cape Town, demanding a withdrawal of Tormin's mining license, due to the company's illegal activities and environmental affronts.

That evolved into a 5-week legal strike of around 200-250 workers in September 2015 when the company announced wage cuts, and an announcement that workers were also expected to work 220 hours per month - 31 hours over the legal upper limit set by legislation.

25 workers were suspended after the strikes, and while workers have been offered new contracts, alarming conditions were stipulated, including the demand they do not join the NUM in exchange for an 8% salary increase.

In their December quarterly report, MRC states:

"The strike activity, as announcement in the previous quarter, abated at the commencement of the December quarter and no further activity or correspondence was received from the National Union of Mineworkers. Given the union membership amongst the Tormin mine site workforce is well below the 50% threshold (currently at ~8%), the union will effectively become derecognised in the March 2016 quarter."

Ground Up, a community publication and joint project with University of Cape Town, reported one employee saying, "Everything was going good before the current people took over. We're mistreated at the mine. The general manager (Australian Gary Thompson), who is 68, swears at us and makes sexual comments to women employees. Accidents with transport at the plant are not reported or investigated.

Gary is not afraid to tell us that if you go inside the mine gates, you're in Australia and if you leave then you're in South Africa. The high-paying positions depend on who you are and how you look."

MRC's links to violence against South Africans dates back to 2003, when a headman at the Xolobeni mine on the Wild Coast was shot dead after criticizing the company, and most recently, were alleged to have been behind the assassination of another anti-MRC mining activist, 'Bazooka' Radebe.

From the pristine beauty of South Africa's Wild Coast on the Indian Ocean, to the devastating and ongoing mining activities on the western Atlantic coast.

The People Shall Govern

Photo: Warrenski

Photo: Sam Nzima

Photo: Samantha Marx

Photo: Meraj Chhaya

South Africa is often referred to as the "protest capital of the world". Since the beginning of the 1900's, people have been taking to the streets for various reasons that create discontent: education in Afrikaans, lack of services, anti-apartheid, high cost of education, labor rights, making marijuana legal, and countless other reasons. There have been reports that as many as 15 protests per day have occurred in some years, many of which go unreported, and it is usually those accompanied by violence which reach headline status.

While civil protests can be traced back to 1913 when black women, struggling under the burden of keeping the agricultural homestead running while their men ventured to the cities to find work as migrant laborers, took to the streets protesting the requirement to carry a pass. Their developing independence and political education created a strength and resilience that increased over the ensuing decades. The notion of the undereducated and submissive African woman was dealt a blow in August, 1956, when around 20,000 protesters marched on the Union Buildings to deliver a petition to the government, demanding the end of the

> *We, women, will never carry these passes. This is something that touches my heart. I appeal to you young Africans to come forward and fight. These passes make the road even narrower for us. We have seen unemployment, lack of accommodation and families broken because of passes. We have seen it with our men. Who will look after our children when we go to jail for a small technical offence -- not having a pass?* – Dora Tamana, January 4, 1953, Langa Township protest

travel document. The event was officially recognized by the South African government in 1994 as seminal enough to warrant a national holiday.

The Women's Charter of 1954 lays out a series of points and goals that remain relevant in the 21st century.

THE WOMEN'S CHARTER

Adopted at the Founding Conference of the Federation of South African Women

Johannesburg, 17 April 1954

Preamble:

We, the women of South Africa, wives and mothers, working women and housewives, African, Indians, European and Coloured, hereby declare our aim of striving for the removal of all laws, regulations, conventions and customs that discriminate against us as women, and that deprive us in any way of our inherent right to the advantages, responsibilities and opportunities that society offers to any one section of the population.

A Single Society:

We women do not form a society separate from the men. There is only one society, and it is made up of both women and men. As women we share the problems and anxieties of our men, and join hands with them to remove social evils and obstacles to progress.

Test of Civilisation:

The level of civilisation which any society has reached can be measured by the degree of freedom that its members enjoy. The status of women is a test of civilisation. Measured by that standard, South Africa must be considered low in the scale of civilised nations.

Women's Lot:

We women share with our menfolk the cares and anxieties imposed by poverty and its evils. As wives and mothers, it falls upon us to make small wages stretch a long way. It is we who feel the cries of our children when they are hungry and sick. It is our lot to keep and care for the homes that are too small, broken and dirty to be kept clean. We know the burden of looking after children and land when our husbands are away in the mines, on the farms, and in the towns earning our daily bread.

We know what it is to keep family life going in pondokkies and shanties, or in overcrowded one-room apartments. We know the bitterness of children taken to lawless ways, of daughters becoming unmarried mothers whilst still at school, of boys and girls growing up without education, training or jobs at a living wage.

Poor and Rich:

These are evils that need not exist. They exist because the society in which we live is divided into poor and rich, into non-European and European. They exist because there are privileges for the few, discrimination and harsh treatment for the many. We women have stood and will stand shoulder to shoulder with our menfolk in a common struggle against poverty, race and class discrimination, and the evils of the colourbar.

National Liberation:

As members of the National Liberatory movements and Trade Unions, in and through our various organisations, we march forward with our men in the struggle for liberation and the defence of the working people. We pledge ourselves to keep high the banner of equality, fraternity and liberty. As women there rests upon us also the burden of removing from our society all the social differences developed in past times between men and women, which have the effect of keeping our sex in a position of inferiority and subordination.

Equality for Women:

We resolve to struggle for the removal of laws and customs that deny African women the right to own, inherit or alienate property. We resolve to work for a change in the laws of marriage such as are found amongst our African, Malay and Indian people, which have the effect of placing wives in the position of legal subjection to husbands, and giving husbands the power to dispose of wives' property and earnings, and dictate to them in all matters affecting them and their children.

We recognise that the women are treated as minors by these marriage and property laws because of ancient and revered traditions and customs which had their origin in the antiquity of the people and no doubt served purposes of great value in bygone times.

There was a time in the African society when every woman reaching marriageable stage was assured of a husband, home, land and security.

Then husbands and wives with their children belonged to families and clans that supplied most of their own material needs and were largely self-sufficient. Men and women were partners in a compact and closely integrated family unit.

Women who Labour:

Those conditions have gone. The tribal and kinship society to which they belonged has been destroyed as a result of the loss of tribal land, migration of men away from the tribal home, the growth of towns and industries, and the rise of a great body of wage-earners on the farms and in the urban areas, who depend wholly or mainly on wages for a livelihood.

Thousands of African women, like Indians, Coloured and European women, are employed today in factories, homes, offices, shops, on farms, in professions as nurses, teachers and the like. As unmarried women, widows or divorcees they have to fend for themselves, often without the assistance of a male relative. Many of them are responsible not only for their own livelihood but also that of their children.

Large numbers of women today are in fact the sole breadwinners and heads of their families.

Forever Minors:

Nevertheless, the laws and practices derived from an earlier and different state of society are still applied to them. They are responsible for their own person and their children. Yet the law seeks to enforce upon them the status of a minor.

Not only are African, Coloured and Indian women denied political rights, but they are also in many parts of the Union denied the same status as men in such matters as the right to enter into contracts, to own and dispose of property, and to exercise guardianship over their children.

Obstacle to Progress:

The law has lagged behind the development of society; it no longer corresponds to the actual social and economic position of women. The law has become an obstacle to progress of the women, and therefore a brake on the whole of society.

This intolerable condition would not be allowed to continue were it not for the refusal of a large section of our menfolk to concede to us women the rights and privileges which they demand for themselves.

We shall teach the men that they cannot hope to liberate themselves from the evils of discrimination and prejudice as long as they fail to extend to women complete and unqualified equality in law and in practice.

Need for Education:

We also recognise that large numbers of our womenfolk continue to be bound by traditional practices and conventions, and fail to realise that these have become obsolete and a brake on progress. It is our duty and privilege to enlist all women in our struggle for emancipation and to bring to them all realisation of the intimate relationship that exists between their status of inferiority as women and the inferior status to which their people are subjected by discriminatory laws and colour prejudices.

It is our intention to carry out a nation-wide programme of education that will bring home to the men and women of all national groups the realisation that freedom cannot be won for any one section or for the people as a whole as long as we women are kept in bondage.

An Appeal:

We women appeal to all progressive organisations, to members of the great National Liberatory movements, to the trade unions and working class organisations, to the churches, educational and welfare organisations, to all progressive men and women who have the interests of the people at heart, to join with us in this great and noble endeavour.

Our Aims

We declare the following aims:

This organisation is formed for the purpose of uniting women in common action for the removal of all political, legal, economic and social disabilities. We shall strive for women to obtain:

• The right to vote and to be elected to all State bodies, without restriction or discrimination.

• The right to full opportunities for employment with equal pay and possibilities of promotion in all spheres of work.

• Equal rights with men in relation to property, marriage and children, and for the removal of all laws and customs that deny women such equal rights.

• For the development of every child through free compulsory education for all; for the protection of mother and child through maternity homes, welfare clinics, creches and nursery schools, in countryside and towns; through proper homes for all, and through the provision of water, light, transport, sanitation, and other amenities of modern civilisation.

• For the removal of all laws that restrict free movement, that prevent or hinder the right of free association and activity in democratic organisations, and the right to participate in the work of these organisations.

• To build and strengthen women's sections in the National Liberatory movements, the organisation of women in trade unions, and through the peoples' varied organisation.

• To cooperate with all other organisations that have similar aims in South Africa as well as throughout the world.

• To strive for permanent peace throughout the world.

WATHINT'ABAFAZI WATHINT'IMBOKODO!

You strike the woman, you strike the rock!

Over the decades, women were consistently at the forefront of the struggle against discrimination. Many went into exile as a result of political pressure, but many more led marches, forming groups like the United Women's Congress in 1981, which raised issues of child care, and increases in bus fares, and food prices. They also campaigned against police brutality, especially as it impacted children. Finding economic boycotts extremely effective, they launched a series of devastating rent and shopping boycotts, withholding their money in an effort to raise attention.

As the country moved towards democracy and the demise of apartheid, women never let up. Their voices were heard in every sphere, demanding their freedom, their rights, and by extension, every South African's freedom and rights.

On Women's Day this year – August 9, 2016 – as the ANC was celebrating and simultaneously dealing with the confusion resulting in a devastating diminishing of their support base, the President stood up to address the nation. Once again, it was the women who, rather than join the opposition party in their usual dramatic walk-out, stood up, silently walked to stand in front of the President's podium, holding signs in powerful protest.

With their backs to President Zuma, he had no idea what was happening, and continued speaking while the crowd started responding, whispering and snapping photographs. The media started to crowd in, and when the confusion finally filtered through to Zuma and he marched off stage, security manhandled the women out of the room.

'Khwezi' has become a symbol of the epidemic of violence against women that sweeps many of South Africa's townships unabated, and filters through into the urban areas, making the country one of the least safe places for women. When Jacob Zuma was accused of raping the woman known as "Khwezi", his defense was that she was wearing a "kanga", and that piece of clothing was clearly an invitation – nay, an obligation - to have sex. A colorful length of printed fabric, worn throughout the continent, and now included in world famous fashion de-signers latest appropriations of Africa, the Kanga had never before been seen as an irresistible invitation to force oneself on a woman, but Zuma's defense worked, and he was acquitted.

Africa Check is a non-profit, independent, media development organization set up in 2012, with offices in Johannesburg, Dakar and London, producing reports in English and French testing claims made by public figures, institutions and the media against the best available evidence, with the goal.to promote accuracy in public debate and the media in Africa and to raise the quality of information available to society across the continent.

To read Africa Check's report on protests in South Africa: "Have protests in South Africa nearly doubled since 2010?", scan the QR code, or find the link on the Perspective Publications website: http://perspective-publications.com

I am Khanga

By Fezekile Ntsukela Kuzwayo (nicknamed 'Khwezi' by the media during the rape trial)

I wrap myself around the curvaceous bodies of women all over Africa

I am the perfect nightdress on those hot African nights

The ideal attire for household chores

I secure babies happily on their mother's backs

Am the perfect gift for new bride and new mother alike

Armed with proverbs, I am vehicle for communication between women

I exist for the comfort and convenience of a woman

But no no no make no mistake …

I am not here to please a man

And I certainly am not a seductress

Please don't use me as an excuse to rape

Don't hide behind me when you choose to abuse

You see

That's what he said my Malume

The man who called himself my daddy's best friend

Shared a cell with him on [Robben] Island for ten whole years

He said I wanted it

That my khanga said it

That with it I lured him to my bed

That with it I want you is what I said

But what about the NO I uttered with my mouth

Not once but twice

And the please no I said with my body

What about the tear that ran down my face as I lay stiff with shock

In what sick world is that sex

In what sick world is that consent

The same world where the rapist becomes the victim

The same world where I become the bitch that must burn

The same world where I am forced into exile because I spoke out

This is NOT my world

I reject that world

My world is a world where fathers protect and don't rape

My world is a world where a woman can speak out

Without fear for her safety

My world is a world where no one , but no one is above the law

My world is a world where sex is pleasurable not painful

The Purple Shall Govern

Photo: Image courtesy: www.sthp.saha.org.za

In the mid-1990's, I visited Cape Town on a brief vacation. Walking around the city, a man passed me wearing a T-shirt that had clearly seen better days, but what struck me was the splotches of purple on it. Our eyes caught, and in silent understanding, we acknowledged the significance of it.

On September 2, 1989, anti-apartheid protesters gathered at the beautiful Greenmarket Square, the historic square built in 1696, home first to a slave market, later a vegetable market, and currently, vendors from all over Africa gather to sell their wares on the worn cobble paving. As with all protests during the dark days of South Africa's 1980's, it was not a "government sanctioned" march – and illegal protests were often dealt with using brutal methods.

Water cannons became popular in breaking up protests, but Cape Town took that to another level. As hundreds of protesters gathered on the Square in a plan to march to Parliament, the bright yellow police vehicles moved in to block the exits at each corner.

Given 10 minutes to disperse, the crowd, well aware that they were trapped, sat down. The police waited 6 minutes before letting loose the cannons, and instead of water, purple dye was aimed at them. Shopkeepers hurriedly closed up, with one rescuing a mother pushing a baby stroller, and the protesters scattered, followed rapidly by police, wielding batons, sjamboks, and tear gas. Many protesters found refuge in the magnificent cathedral on the square, but one man, Phillip Ivey, commandeered a police vehicle, turning the cannon on the police and the headquarters of the ruling National Party.

Archbishop Desmond Tutu negotiated for the release of more than 50 local and international journalists, as well as around 500 protesters, with courts working through the night to process everyone.

The following day, graffiti was seen in numerous places around the city, "The Purple Shall Govern", and for years afterwards, the intention of the police to easily identify the protesters backfired in a citizenry proudly wearing their stained T-shirts.

Right:

The 10-storey, 2,174 ft2 (201.6 m2) "Purple Shall Govern" Mandela mural, in Braamfontein, Johannesburg. The first African artwork by American street artist, Shepard Fairey, it was completed in September 2014 to mark the 25th anniversary of the Purple Rain Protest.

Artist: Shepard Fairey

In honor of the September, 1989 Purple Rain protest, South African folk singer-song-writer, Edi Niederlander, shared these lyrics.

STILL DEMANDING

loose in the city, see the dancing feet
see the dogs and the military line the street
clenched in anger, see the fists of rage,
still demanding a living wage.

my friend, please don't leave me here cause the night has begun
the road's on fire and the flames grow higher
and there's no place to run.

see the teargas tumble, see the bullets fly,
see them run and stumble and the price is high.
hear the screaming sirens, hear the thud of the gun,
all these years of violence, must be undone, must be undone.

my friend, please don't leave me here cause the night has begun
the road's on fire and the flames grow higher
and there's no place to run.

pens are lifted, more self-serving lies,
while down on the ground, one more person dies.
see the black smoke rising, see it rise from the sand,
saying the time for vengeance is now at hand
time is at hand...

album "Reflections from Pre-Liberation South Africa"
© circa 1990. Words & music: edi niederlander

Senegal has an estimated 50,000 street children as young as 3-years old, who are brought hundreds of kilometres to the capital of Dakar, ostensibly for religious education, but who are largely caught up in human trafficking and slavery. Sending their children to a "marabout" or spiritual guide, alleviates the financial struggles of many families from Senegal, Guinea-Bissau, Mali and Guinea. The boys are forced to work the streets, begging for money, food, clothing. The girls are kept within the daaras to do household chores, and care for the animals.

Islam encourages the giving of alms, thus providing a form of cover for the marabouts, and by extension, a reluctance by the government to do anything about the situation.

After a tragic fire in 2013 which killed 9 children in one daara, human rights groups stepped up their efforts in putting pressure on the Senegalese government. In response, the President announced a ban on all children begging on the streets, and declared that all non-Senegalese children be repatriated. That order had to be rescinded as violence erupted in Mali and Guinea-Bissau, and the child-free streets only lasted a few days.

The main routes of migration in Senegal and Guinea-Bissau for boys in Quranic boarding schools marked by forced child begging.

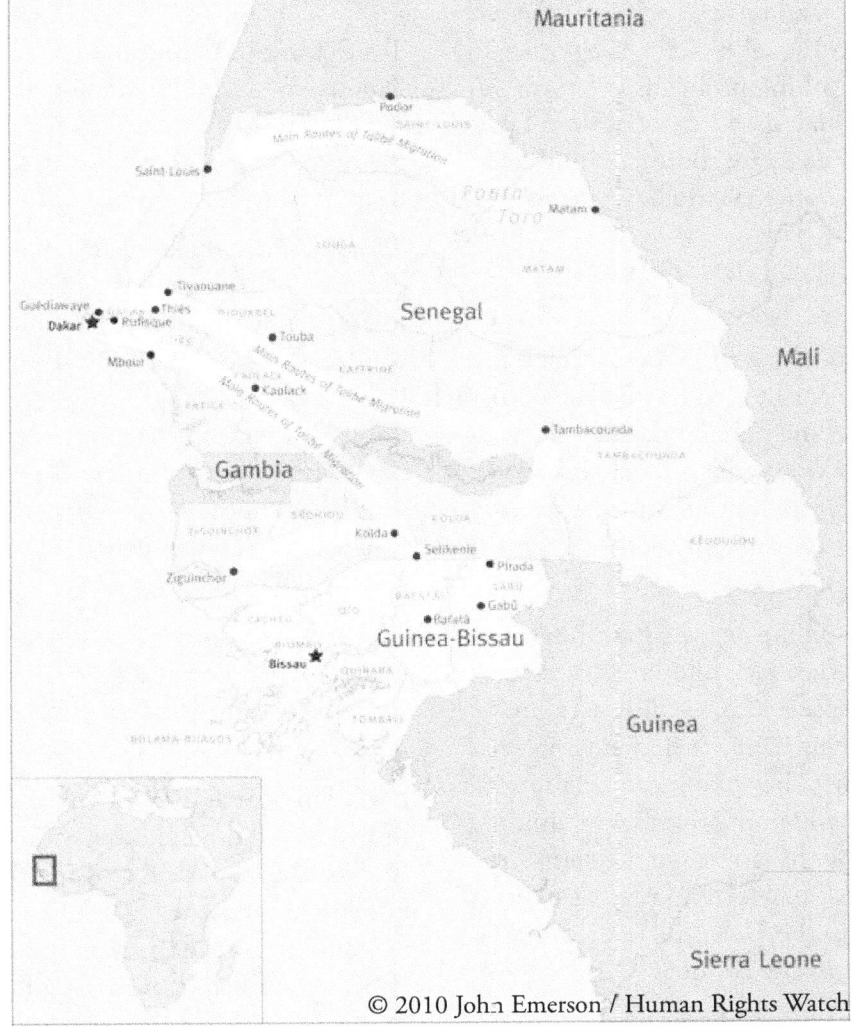

© 2010 John Emerson / Human Rights Watch

Talibes
Modern Day Slaves

TEXT and PHOTOS by Mario Cruz
In collaboration with FotoEvidence

The *Talibes* and the *Daaras*

Talibe is an Arabic term for disciple. What was once a respectable education system has become criminal. What tries to pass as religious teaching today has become a business for exploiting children. Everyday, *talibes*, who range in age from five to 15 years old, beg on the streets for eight hours a day and return back to an overcrowded and squalid *daara*, rife with skin disease, breathing problems, stomach parasites and Malaria. Little education takes place and *talibes* are routinely subjected to physical abuse. Mario Cruz gained rare access to the dark and violent world of the *daaras* where children's dreams are suffocated by fear.

The physical abuse of *talibes* is well known but takes place hidden behind the doors of the *daaras*. The *marabouts* are well aware that their actions are criminal and access to *daaras* is heavily restricted by them. Even the police have difficulty getting access to some *daaras*.

Talibes are unlike beggars found in other countries. They are children with marks of physical abuse and often visibly traumatized. But Senegalese society doesn't seem to see them. They have become a routine part of daily life. The number of children exploited by this system of modern-day slavery is estimated to number as many as 30,000 in the Dakar region alone and 50,000 across the country.

The long tradition of sending boys to study at Quranic boarding schools in Senegal is rooted in positive values of religious and moral education but in the last decade the system has changed drastically and uncontrollably. Thousands of so-called teachers use religious education as a cover for economic exploitation of the children in their charge. With many of them having more than one *daara* throughout Senegal.

Trafficking in Children

Parents often send their children to study the Quran because they simply can't afford their education, others just believe that a *daara* is still a good solution.

Today, child trafficking also plays a crucial part in the numbers. Most of the *talibes* are Senegalese but the number of children from neighboring countries, like Guinea-Bissau, has grown to become an important part of this phenomenon. Every month, the Guinean anti-trafficking unit finds children in remote areas between Senegal and Guinea-Bissau.

The children know that their only escape is to cross the border to Guinea-Bissau because when they ask for help in Senegal, most of the time they are sent back to the *daaras*.

Earlier in March 2015, Guinea-Bissau authorities found 54 children hidden inside five vehicles that were crossing the border to Senegal but Senegalese authorities have failed to prosecute the traffickers. Several Guinean families are asking for help so that their children can be found and

Above: A young talibe bound by chains in an isolation area of a daara in the city of Touba, May 27, 2015. In this daara the youngest talibes are shackled by their ankles to stop them from trying to run away. The chains length only allows them to use an improvised bathroom in a separate area of the daara. These children can stay like this for days, weeks, even months until they gain the marabout's trust. Their guardian explains, "When I release them, I give them the freedom to beg like the rest of the talibes."

Below: Talibes sleep together inside a daara in Saint Louis, in northern Senegal, May 21, 2015. The daara, with over 30 children, has no clean water and barely any electricity. Often, the children sleep on the concrete floor without any protection.

Above: Guinean military police approaches a group of children walking through a forest area near Bissau border, GuineaBissau, June 15, 2015. Earlier in March 2015.

Below: Children that used to be talibes cool off at SOS Talibe Center in Bafata, Guinea-Bissau, June 8, 2015. The Center received 45 cases of talibes returning from Senegal in 2014. Some of them ran away from daaras but others were handed over to the authorities by Marabouts when brought to the courts.

rescued.

Guinean military forces are facing this problem as one of the country's top priorities. At this time there are controls at the exits of cities and is impossible to leave the capital Bissau with a child without a written authorization from the parents. Still, the *marabout* power is well rooted within the peripheral countries to Senegal which makes the traffic difficult to control.

Ineffective Enforcement

Though Senegal adopted a law in 2005 prohibiting forced begging and child trafficking, only a handful of cases have been prosecuted.

In July 2015, the government's anti-trafficking unit took its first census of over 1,000 Quranic schools but the unit lacks the resources to check every *daara*, and the police don't know exactly how many of them exist. The *daaras* are unregulated, set up in abandoned buildings and unfinished construction projects. The Senegalese parliament has yet to pass a law regulating these schools, and does not have a scheduled date for discussion. Every year on April 20, the country observes National Talibe Day and the issue of *talibes* comes up for discussion but, year after year, little progress is made.

Since 2010, just one exploitative Quranic teacher has been convicted and sentenced to one month in prison, under the anti-trafficking law. The lack of reporting abuses to authorities is rooted in the low awareness across Senegalese society about how to handle trafficking and forced begging.

Unfortunately the current budgetary support does not account for the extra capacity and resources needed to close schools that violate the law's standards and find appropriate shelter for children while mediating their return to their families.

Following heightened media attention on

child begging in Senegal in 2010, thirteen Quranic teachers were convicted for forcing children to beg under the 2005 anti-trafficking law. But 12 were given six-month suspended sentences and fines of $160, well below the minimum penalties.

The Life of a *Talibe*

"Every day I try not to cry. Every day I try not to scream. I don't sleep. I just close my eyes and imagine myself in a different place. I don't know who my family is, I just know that I'm not from here...I'm tired of being beaten, even when I have the money I get beaten. I know stories about dead talibes but I'm not afraid of death anymore." Amadou is 15 years old.

Inside a *daara* each *talibe* has a different posture, some are crying, some are fighting the tiredness, some are silent, but they all tremble with fear. Most of them don't know where they came from or who their families are. The only thing they know is violence. The youngest boys often are shackled to stop them from trying to run away.

It's getting harder every day for all *talibes* to keep up with their guardians' demands. More *talibes* on the streets means less money for each one. They know that it will be impossible to collect the amount of money imposed by the *marabout* and that means only one thing: punishment.

The demands of *marabouts* are growing as more money is demanded even as the number of *talibes* grow and in the face of the limited resources of people in Senegal. Not only the amount of money required is increasing, but also the *marabout* demands are changing, with some of them using

Below: Demba Fati, 14, outside the medical support room of Mason de La Gare center in St. Louis, Senegal, May 20, 2015. His Marabout beat him with an iron rod after he tried to escape.

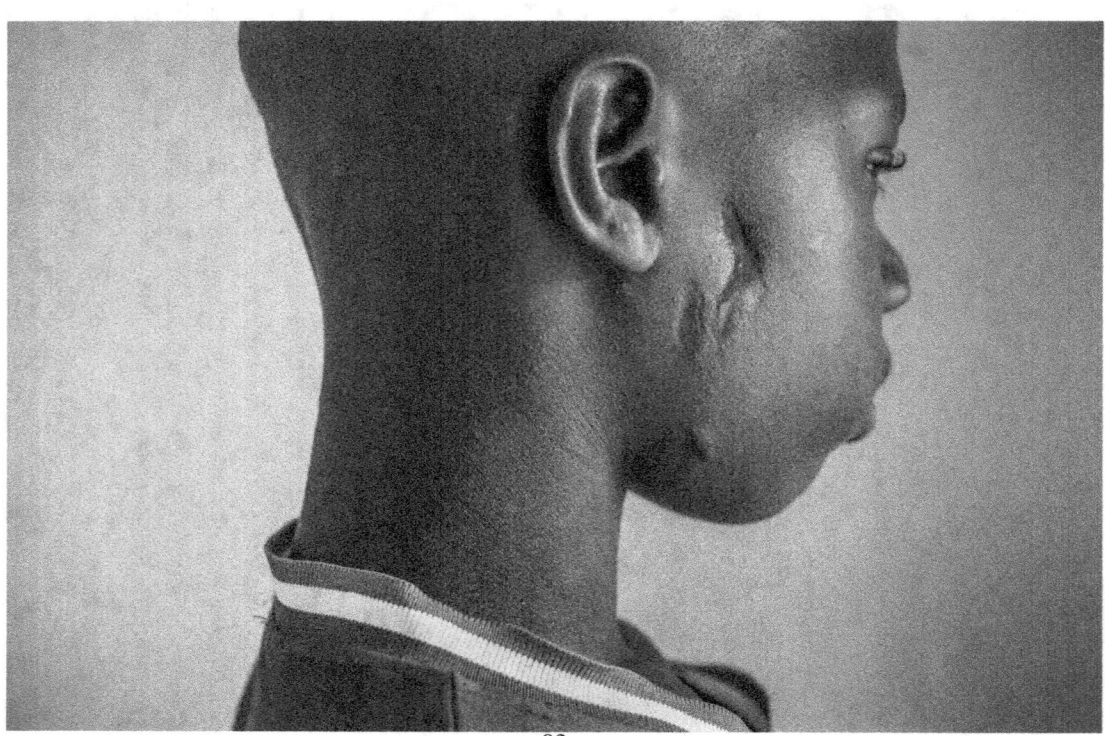

Above: Abdoulaye, 15, imprisoned in one room of a daara in the Diamaguene area, city of Thies, Senegal, May 18, 2015. The rooms have windows with security bars to keep the talibes from running away.

Below: A talibe begs in a bridge in the city of Thies, Senegal. Many of them spend their days almost without eating and end up sleeping on the street out of fatigue.

talibes as cheap labor for different kinds of services or forcing them to dig for valuable goods in large garbage dumps around cities.

Sadly, many of these children can stay enslaved for many years in a long a dramatic path towards despair, but some of them flee and take a chance living on the street. Some of them become what they hated most when they reach adolescence in a horrible cycle that infects Senegalese society.

Editorial Update: In July and August, 2016, efforts by the government to clamp down on begging resulted in more than 500 children being taken off the streets, and authorities are working to locate their families. The President has announced that parents, marabouts and Quaranic teachers who are found to be abusing children, will be prosecuted.

Above: Ibrahima Ndao, marabout of a daara in Rufisque, whips a talibe child after he makes a mistake reading an excerpt of the Quran, May 17, 2015. The talibes are subjected to physical violence when they fail to get the daily quota imposed by the marabout or if they make a mistake while reading the Quran.

The Power of the Lens

My purpose in this project has been to alert the world to this systematic exploitation and abuse of children and bring back documentary evidence that would demand a response from the international community.

In July 2009, I was in Guinea-Bissau when I first heard stories about Guinean children who were taken to Senegal to work and beg for Quranic teachers. Many of them had disappeared while playing in remote areas; others were given by their parents after promises made by *marabouts*. These stories stayed with me.

In early 2015, I started planning an in-depth project about what was happening in Senegal. I made contact with Human Rights Watch, Senegal's Ministry of Justice and local NGO's focused on the *talibes*, like *Voices of Talibes*. I thought I was ready to document the disturbing reality of child slaves but, in truth, I could never be fully prepared to see children whipped and chained in front of me.

After six months of research and investigation, I traveled to Senegal and gained access to several *daaras* across the country: in Dakar, Rufisque, Keuer Massar, Diamaguene, Saint Louis and Touba, where I also followed the lives of many *talibes* that had run away. After Senegal, I went to Guinea Bissau, to visit shelters, families and border points to track the child trafficking that fed some of the *daaras*.

Despite the magnitude of the *talibe* system, I strongly believe that by reporting and sharing the suffering of so many children we can bring needed attention to this problem and change to the criminal and exploitative *talibes* system in Senegal.

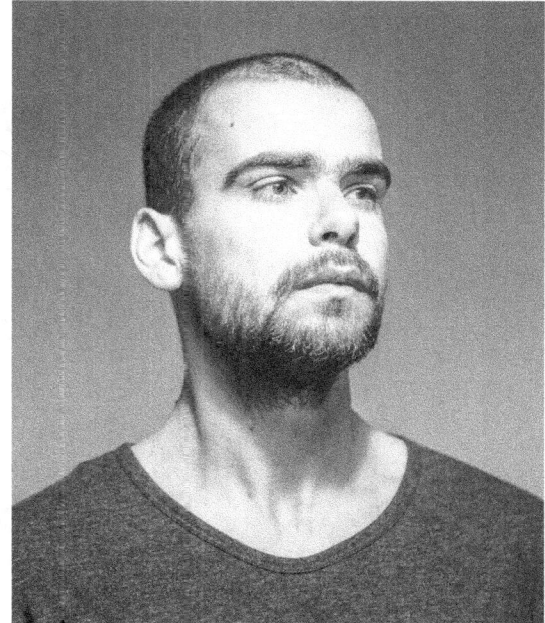

About Mario Cruz

Born in 1987, in Lisbon, Portugal. Mario Cruz studied Photojournalism at Cenjor -Professional School of Journalism. In 2006 he began working with LUSA –Portuguese News Agency / EPA –European Pressphoto Agency.

Since 2012, he has been focused on his personal projects dedicated to social justice and human rights. After publishing the first series of *"Talibes, Modern-day Slaves"* he won World Press Photo -1stPrize for Contemporary Issues (Stories) raising international awareness and pressuring the Senegalese government to address the issue.

Purchase the book at the FotoEvidence bookstore by scanning the QR code, or visiting the "Links" page on the Perspective Publications website.

2017
FotoEvidence
BOOK
AWARD

deadline January 15th 2017
fotoevidence.com

About FotoEvidence
FotoEvidence was founded in 2010 by Svetlana Bachevanova with the intention of publishing the work of documentary photographers working on long-term projects that focus on social justice and human rights. In addition, each year the FotoEvidence Book Award publishes a book for one photographer whose project demonstrates courage and commitment in the pursuit of human rights.

FotoEvidence's website: http://www.fotoevidence.com

The Founding Of Cape Town

by Patric Tariq Mellet

Bo-Kaap, Cape Town

Photo: David Stanley

The other day I was browsing through some old books at a good second-hand bookstore near where I live and found a very interesting statistic in a maritime history book, "THE CAPE OF GOOD HOPE – A MARITIME HISTORY" by Robin Knox-Johnston, concerning the fact that over the full span of the 1600s over 1770 Dutch ships alone had called at the Cape. Although I have done much research and writing on alternative Cape history -it again hit me like a thunderbolt as to how much we were fed a load of bull-dust as history during Apartheid times, and I will explain why.

Now I have always been interested in maritime affairs. I went on a working trip to sea for a couple of weeks as an engine-room boy when I was 14, and a number of my family were seamen all their lives. It was one way of getting away from Apartheid South Africa for many men of colour and a means of seeing the world. For 18 months of my five years as a senior officer in the Immigration and Border Control services, I was put in charge of a transformation programme involving modernisation and security upgrade of all SA harbours. I was responsible for pushing for the re-building of a cruise-liner terminal and inter-agency security command centre in Duncan Dock as a pilot to be rolled out for each of our 8 harbours. At the time my vision and intervention was opposed by all and sundry and most vociferously by the Democratic Alliance-controlled City and Province. The narrow view held of preserving the then current business interests within the Waterfront, made them myopic to my vision of taking Cape Town harbour forward as a secure and dynamic gateway into South Africa. The manner in which my former opponents talk now has opportunistically changed – they all want to claim responsibility for what they now see as a great addition to Cape Town's offerings. Such is life and so too is our past often skewed. I love the sea and Cape Town harbour and the maritime trade has a long and fascinating history. So what has all this maritime stuff got to do with the warping of history, you might justifiably ask?

I came home after my jaunt at the bookshop and did some quick research by consulting a work – "The Dutch East India Company's Shipping 1602 – 1795 in a comparative perspective" by FS Gaastra and JR Bruijn from Leiden University. I wanted to verify the statistic that I found and to interrogate it some more. This work considers all the variables at play for each decade of two centuries and provides the statistics for six European powers merchant fleets during the 1600s and 1700s between Europe and South and Southeast Asia. It shows us that just over the period 1590 until 1700 there were 2,632 ships that had to call at the Cape and - here is the thing - before van Riebeeck arrived in 1652, the figure of ships that called at the Cape was 1,071.

This represented a rise from around 8 ships a year in the last decade of the 1500s to around 30 in a year with layovers of 2 days to 8 days by the time Jan van Riebeeck arrived. So hey, wait a minute. Table Bay was quite a busy port for at least four decades before van Riebeeck arrived. Why then did he and historians looking back at his contribution give us a scenario that said the rather ignorant and good-for-nothing locals were awestruck at van Riebeeck's arrival and that he set up the first refreshment operations, no thanks to the locals?

The Dutch dominated the numbers of ships doing lay-overs and then England followed with France, Portugal, Denmark also regularly coming to the Cape. Interestingly, in the period 1610 to 1620 English ships increased to ten times the number of the previous decade. This strongly indicates why the English considered colonization at this point in time and then later opted to support local development of indigene

CAPE TOWN AND TABLE BAY IN 1714.   [To face page 153.

Above: Image taken from "Illustrated Official Handbook of the Cape and South Africa. A résumé of the history, conditions, populations, productions, and resources of the several colonies, states, and territories. Edited by John Noble. [With a map.]", Courtesy British Library

support infrastructure.

Indicators of the progression of the English approach is to study their actions of first taking Chief Xhore of the Goringhaiqua to London for training and orientation in 1613; the failure of their Newgate convict settlement at the Cape in 1614 – 17; the taking of Chief Autshumao to Jakarta (Batavia) in 1630; the subsequent establishment of an indigene refreshment station on Robben Island in 1632; and the subsequent move of this project to the Camissa River on the Table Bay Mainland by 1638.

This English-sponsored relationship with Autshumao and his 60-strong Goringhaicona permanently settled alongside the Camissa (//Gam i Ssa) river and beach continued over 20 years before the arrival of Jan van Riebeeck and represents the true foundation of the town which would become the City of Cape Town.

Autshumao was dealing with 2 to 3 ships per month at this stage and their stay-overs would be anything between two days and more than a week. Effectively, there was an almost daily presence of European visitors. This represents a very different picture to one of Jan van Riebeeck arriving to greet a desolate Cape and just a bunch of beach scavenging ignorant indigenous people awestruck at seeing Europeans. In fact, the fleet that brought Jan van Riebeeck back to the Netherlands from Vietnam had stayed over in Table Bay for 18 days.

As I looked through more maritime texts I found fairly glowing accounts of his services and that of other Khoena. Each European power seemed to have had their own trusted man who performed a range of tasks including keeping mail and passing it on to other ships. Ships had even developed a gun-signal protocol for summonsing their hired hands.

But let's stop and look at some of the dynamics of the Dutch and other European shipping of this magnitude. Let's also look at the probable impact on the Khoena and then let us also keep in mind the improbability of the cock 'n bull history that has been handed down to us over the years, with the collaboration of our academic institutions.

When one locks at the comparative maritime records of that time, one gets a good picture of the competitiveness of the European/English powers, the dominance of the Dutch, the size and shape of their vessels and changes over time to this technology due to the cargoes carried. One also has to look at what was driving the increase in shipping to South and Southeast Asia and the dynamics of that region. What were these ships carrying to that part of the world and why so frequently? One also sees a dramatic and striking attrition rate of ships by examining the return journeys. The attrition rate through wrecks and wear-and-tear on vessels shows that only around 50% of these vessels returned to Europe. It spurred on the development of shipbuilding technology and the need for advanced stop-over stations en route.

The attrition rate was the driver for the need for sophisticated stop-over points starting with refreshment posts and graduating to ship repair facilities. The records also show an almost studious omission in our history books to mention that the main outward bound role of the shipping was to take company officials and huge loads of troops to supply the wars in South and South East Asia with soldiers. There the Dutch were fighting the English and Portuguese and Muslim Sultanates and they needed to fortify their factories and huge bases in India, Sri Lanka and at Batavia. Factories stretched across the long Indian and Bengal Coast and from Arakan (Rhakine) in Myanmar, to Thailand, Cambodia, Vietnam, Malaysia, through to Formosa, and Japan and then throughout Indonesia.

This was a scenario thirsty for thousands of armed troops. The United Dutch East India Company had all the powers of state ceded to them by the Dutch States General. Now here's another thing – these troops needed time ashore at strategic stops. The voyages were long and soldiers and officials got sick and died, but also grew grumpy and fights broke out. It was most certain that by 1615, the troops had to have had time ashore at the Cape of Good Hope.

The English took the lead in trying to find a solution to further developing the port. The English East India Company under Lord Thomas Smythe came up with an elaborate plan to establish a small trading colony using freed convicts from Newgate prison. They also knew that they would need to co-operate with the indigene population, and took Chief Xhore of the Goringhaiqua to London, Pocohontas style, so that he could be orientated to their requirements. Chief Xhore was returned to Table Bay, and 10 convicts under Captains Peyton and Crosse came out to start up a settlement.

The whole thing fell apart in three years. But then the English followed plan B – by using the services of Xhore as a point man who served the French, Portuguese and Danes as well. He ably facilitated trade and the other needs of the Europeans. He was more reluctant to serve the Dutch, and at one time pointedly refused because they had behaved abusively to his people. For this, Xhore lost his life at Dutch hands around 1626. The English had so come to rely on Xhore (whom they called Cary) that they found the need to establish a new point person. This is how in around 1630/31 Autshumao (whom they called Harry) was taken for orientation to Jakarta and then returned to the Cape. The English assisted Autshumao on two occasions to first establish himself formally as a trader-facilitator for passing shipping, initially on Robben Island and then later at the Camissa River on the mainland – roughly near the end of the Grand Parade where the Golden Acre Centre now stands.

There are many signs that Autshumao performed his trader and port master roles ably, was a proficient linguist, was shrewd and astute and also knew the value of playing off English against their enemies, the Dutch. The large formations of Khoena also knew to keep their main herds of thousands of cattle and sheep and their families far inland, away from the Europeans, so Autshumao was not simply an opportunist go-between trader but served a very useful defensive buffer role.

Now what is the impact of the big numbers of ships, the frequency of these ships visiting the Cape, the different nationalities involved, the need for repairs stop overs, the need for soldiers and officials to go ashore in large numbers, the problems on the ships, the need for supplies, probable occasional need to leave the sick behind, the required postal and news services and so on?

The first thing that it should tell one is that Table Bay at the Cape was already a Port before 1652. Secondly, it was already a trading and layover station.

Then, from my own experience of working in harbours and resolving the problems that arise, this kind of sea traffic creates stowaways and stay-behinds; shore-leave by men leads to sexual encounters and relations becoming a norm of port; ship repairs would have needed the gathering of repair materials and therefore negotiation of terrain, cutting and gathering timber

Above: Possible location of the VOC ship 'De Nieuwe Haerlem' (1647). The area is in the intertidal, between Milnerton and Blauwbergstrand, Western Cape Province.
Courtesy: South African Heritage Resources Agency (SAHRA)

and this would have led to job creation and further trade.

This amount of sea-transport and human traffic must have had a huge impact on the local population living at the small Camissa settlement. The people in this indigene settlement were a recent phenomenon of maroons from other clans coming together – most probably as result of social impacts brought about through the visiting ships. All of the historical materials that I have read together with the size of the shipping stop-overs at the Cape and the vast numbers on board those ships and the poor state of those vessels when put alongside the information that we know of the social

history of the Khoena between 1590 and 1652, suggest that we have all been taken for a ride by historians of the colonial and Apartheid eras.

Pause now for a minute.

In 1647, a shipwreck occurred at Table Bay. The Dutch ship Nieuwe Haarlem on its way back to Holland was wrecked at Woodstock beach. The survivors under Captain Leendert Janszen built a small wood and sand fort called Sandenburg at Salt River and built a deep well for underground fresh water. They remained at the Cape for a year until 1648. Leendert Janszen, Matthew Proot and Jodocus

Hondius III (a scientist), used their time to gather intelligence on the terrain, the indigenes and the other visiting vessels as well as mapping Table Bay.

A fleet of 12 ships that stopped over for 18 days, under the command of Admiral GW de Jong, took Janzsen and his 62 men back to Holland. On board the same ship carrying Captain Janzsen was a certain disgraced VOC merchant – Jan van Riebeeck - who showed a deep interest in Janzsen's proposition that the Dutch should establish a permanent base at Table Bay.

Van Riebeeck had been fired from his job in Hanoi (Tonkin) in Vietnam because he was cheating the VOC (Dutch Vereenigde Oost-Indische Compagnie, known in English as the Dutch East India Company) by insider trading. He was ordered to return to Holland and this was his voyage of disgrace. On board this return voyage, Janzsen and his five senior men prepared a proposal – "remonstrantie" - to the VOC.

Van Riebeeck, to redeem himself with the VOC, offered to lead a settlement expedition to establish Dutch control at the Cape. The Dutch needed to maintain their dominance in the east and hence the control of the strategically positioned Cape was seen as vital and that there needed to be a more technologically advanced port operation to achieve the much needed ship repair and servicing required.

Janzsen and de Jong's views of the indigenes was a lot more favourable and respectful that that of Jan van Riebeeck and his later approach. Their approach mirrored that of the English of establishing cooperative relations. Janzsen spoke glowingly of the Khoena in Table Bay who were of great assistance to him during his long sojourn. He recommended that the VOC accept and respect the trading and servicing role of the indigenes by ensuring that any settlement is based on cooperation rather than conquest. Van Riebeeck, however, was bent on conquest and dislodging any form of intermediary trading by indigenes. He wanted a simple direct trading relationship as a stepping stone for company control over resources. As such, the Camissa community's entrepreneurial approach of a proto-trading class of local people of colour was out of the question for van Riebeeck. He was also wary of the fact that the local kingpin, Autshumao, had a very strong relationship with the English.

The report to the VOC presented the statistics of how many vessels were stopping over, how many people going ashore, the trade that was being done, and importantly, that no European power had established themselves at the Port, where trading was only organised by the indigenes under an English trained and sympathetic Autshumao and a relatively small settled group of indigene 'Watermans' next to the Camissa - which they called the Soetwater Stroom (also known as Rio Dolce, Rio de Camis and Platteklipstroom). Van Riebeeck saw this scenario as a push-over and thus the die was cast. The VOC and Captain Janzsen had their ideas, but van Riebeeck had his own. The infamous 'Skelm of Vietnam' was not about to change his old habits.

History has been most unfair to Autshumao and the Goringhaicona trading mission at Camissa and has never properly analysed what happened in the 50 years prior to van Riebeeck's arrival, or the 20-year old human trading settlement at Camissa, and the impacts of the large scale visitations of ships, sailors, officials and troops who were adequately catered for by locals. The social history of this port village with its sizable yet relatively small population had changed their mode of living, economic and social habits as happened in every other port across the African coastline.

This criminal negligence in academia which continues to this day has to be challenged. Indigenes are treated as anthropological and archaeological subjects in the paradigm of stone-age and iron-age peoples, rather than as subjects of social history enquiry by our museums and educational institutions. This has not only robbed us of the ability to properly assess our past, but has also fed into a primitivistic paradigm in terms of how many who seek to revive the memory of and understanding of our forebears think about and represent our forebears today in an equally skewed manner. European historical evaluation, which is highly skewed, sets the edges of discourse today and all sorts of European overlays from feudal monarchies to modern nation concepts are placed on our past and then misinforms our present.

Today, we have people who claim to be indigene kings seeking recognition for numerous kingdoms or as a nation or nations. From what I can gather, there were no hereditary chiefs or kings, but rather elders recognised by their communities as such because of leadership and achievement. Both Xhore and Autshumao became recognised as chiefs or leaders because of their achievements and their people's recognition thereof, rather than were born to be such. Autshumao's niece Krotoa is one of my 9th great grandmothers and if I were to believe some of today's overlays of royalty on our past then I would be a prince. I harbour no such desire to covet an erroneous royal persona, but I do have a pride in the achievements of both Autshumao and Krotoa.

The early foundational human endeavour of a Khoena settled trading community which embraced visitors, and whom no doubt some visitors embraced and remained and assimilated into, certainly would have had offspring, as occurs in all ports. This element of children born from relations between the sea-travelling Europeans requires much, much more research and evaluation attention. This Camissa (//Gam i Ssa) village where the Grand Parade, Castle and District Six stands today on the Cape Peninsula known to the Khoena as //Hui Gaeb! can give us all a whole new take on our past. It is the Camissa Footprint and all that was born out of this pre-1652 and post-1652 that informs our sense of identity.

We certainly cannot ignore the overwhelming evidence that 1652 was not a magical date of Khoena and European interaction….. nor can we ignore the vast numbers of vessels and people from abroad who came here and interacted with locals. Nor can we ignore that key notable indigene figures had travelled abroad and returned and engaged with new technology and trading and new ways of living and were not merely ignorant beach scavengers. With all of this information at our fingertips, we cannot accept uncritically the European writings that have marginalised and robbed us of a fair view of our forebears. Many of the basic assumptions that we make about the past are called into question. We are the descendants of this Camissa footprint as much as we are of the older Khoena modes of living and of slaves brought to this port from elsewhere in Africa, India and Southeast Asia and including all the interactions and resistance proceeding from this site.

We know that across the Peninsula there were up to 40,000 indigene inhabitants, mainly Khoena and over the broader Western Cape up to 50,000 more, both Khoena and San, making up around 16 Khoena clan groupings and at least five San or /Xam groupings of different strengths, and they were very rich in livestock. Van Riebeeck left a record of less known correspondence, other than his famous diaries. While the latter tended to portray him favourably by his own hand, a more wider view of his correspondence and the views of others sheds a different light on the man. It also shows that he laid the foundations for the 160 years of wars that lead to the flight of the Cape Khoena to the northwestern Gariep district and to the mass genocide of the San despite their valiant wars of resistance.

Shortly after arriving at the Cape, Van Riebeeck in 1653 wrote to the VOC imploring them to allow him to round up all the Peninsula Khoena, put them in chains and force them into labour. The VOC refused his request. Then in 1657, he again wrote to the VOC outlining a plan and seeking approval to build 5 'redoubts' in Hout Bay to form concentration camps into which he would lure the Peninsula Khoena and their cattle and then keep them so imprisoned so that they may continuously be forced to supply cattle to the company. This concept was initially considered by the VOC but was rejected only because it would have cost too much and required many soldiers. This, however, was the com-

The two Jan Van Riebeck's.
The handsome devil on the right, immortalised on the old South African currency (pre-1994), was discovered by a geneologist in 1984 to be a Dutch man, Bartholomeus Vermuyden. The portrait was painted by Dirck Craey and is now in the possession of Amsterdam's Rijksmuseum. The real Jan van Riebeeck is on the left.

plete opposite to the approach that Captain Janzsen had promoted. Van Riebeeck's ideas set the paradigm of European- Indigene relations that has remained to this day. Forced removals and the "redoubt" concept, otherwise known as group-areas and reservations, lasted well after Jan van Riebeeck, right up to the imposition of the Group Areas Act under Apartheid.

There was much that was phony about the "skelm from Vietnam" and perhaps it all came together in the biggest con-trick pulled on all South Africans in the 20th century. The political ideological skewing of history came full circle when an image of van Riebeeck and his wife was popularised. This image of a handsome, wavy-haired and immaculately groomed Dutch gentleman was presented to us as statues, images on coins and banknotes, stamps and in pageants. It was as plastic as the historical yarn that we were fed. In the 1990s, we learnt that this was not van Riebeeck at all, nor was the image of van Riebeeck's wife genuine – that of Maria de la Quellerie. The original paintings are in a museum in the Netherlands and are of a certain Mr Vermuyden and his mistress Ms Kettering. A real painting was found of the aging Jan van Riebeeck who just did not have the looks for a romantic founder. The plagiarised images are deeply embedded in the minds of South Africans and mirrors the skewed history and heritage that many still hold dear. This stymies our ability to move on as people in the South Africa of today.

Likewise the "Skelm from Vietnam" was not quite the pious man, either. Historian Mansell Upham tells us that while formally he forbade European company officials for having "carnal conversation" (sexual intercourse) with slaves and indigenes, privately he is on record as telling officials to go forth and "fruitify" them.

There are much more complexities in our past than many care to acknowledge, but also a wonderful focal point arises for us to move away from racial terminology and exclusive terminology in anchoring our local identities alongside our national, regional and pan-African identities. My inquiry and studies looking at that first Goringhaicona port community at Camissa, make me proud to call myself Camissa, and proudly African before anything else. My 9th great-grandmother Krotoa, Autshumao's niece, and another of my 9th great-grandmother's was a young slave Lijsbeth Arabus. Both worked for the van Riebeeck family. I live in a place called South Africa within borders made by imperialism and colonialism. I am passionate about Southern Africa and Africa and I am proudly African. I am driven in this by my local heritage rooted in all that arises out of the Camissa footprint founded on the indigene experience at the river village and further enhanced by generations of indigenes, enslaved peoples and non-conform

Photo: Cape Argus

ist Europeans who had children together.

The people of Camissa embraced and assisted the enslaved brought to our shores and these enslaved peoples embraced Camissa. In my family tree there are 24 slaves, 4 Khoena including Krotoa from the Goringhaicona at Camissa as well as an array of European and Afro-Europeans. Camissa is meaningful….not the racial tag of 'Coloured' that was forced on us as an Apartheid badge of identity and which says nothing. Indeed, it is high time too that we stopped racialising our terminology. The state and all of us need to drop using terms like – Coloured, White, and Black to refer to our people. There are three broad heritages that flow through people in South Africa and no rigid walls separating us – African, Afro-European and Afro-Asian. This is heritage and not race. The African family of communities is as diverse as the Afro-European and Afro-Asian heritages.

As Africans, we as Camissa (not Coloured) take our rightful place alongside Zulu, Xhosa, Khoena, San (/Xam), Sotho, Korana, Tswana, Venda, Pedi, Nama, Griqua, Shangaan, Ndebele, Lembe, Swazi and others. We have many sub-community identities in the South African family of African diversity. Imposed 'race' identities are nonsense and divisive. I have always been amazed that all writings on the early people of the Cape only look at the Khoena (Khoi) people through a lens of primitivism as stone and early iron-age people. Very little effort is made to present a social history of these our African forebears or their civilisation.

Over the last 30 years or so, as an amateur historian and heritage activist, I have sought to shed a bit of light on some of the pointers that make up what can be called the history and heritage that falls between the cracks, most especially in terms of both indigene history and that of Cape Slavery.

From just little bits of information, such as the statistic that I happened upon in the bookshop, over these last 30 years, a very different scenario presented itself to me about the founding of Cape Town as a port. None of the information that I put out there is really new. Very little is primary research. Much of the information lays buried, or even not so buried, in the research of others. The information is just being viewed with different eyes and written up with a different perspective and then brought out for view by a non-academic audience.

Also, most of our history is about the outside gaze on Africa and the Cape and its indigenous people…. I am presenting a perspective which dares to look at what happens when you start to look from the Cape shore –from the inside looking outward.

For many years now, I have pointed out a number of things that should get us thinking differently about this past. We need to factor into our thinking that there was European and other visitation for at least 200 years before 1652 and, also numerous historical accounts show us that Phoenicians, Arabs, Javanese and Chinese were on our shores as visitors from 600BC in a continuum to 1421 when the Chinese rounded the Cape and circumnavigated the world. Now here is some other exploration just waiting to be done – and what impacts did these have in the shaping of local social history? Some things too may well remain a mystery.

MediaStorm

WE CREATE CINEMATIC NARRATIVES

MediaStorm is an award-winning multimedia production studio, working with top visual storytellers, interactive designers and global organizations to create cinematic narratives that speak to the heart of the human condition.

MediaStorm collaborates with a diverse range of clients and is training the next generation of storytellers, teaching them how to harness the power of this craft and to engage and inspire viewers.

Food Security In A Changing World

by Leigh Barrett

Photo courtesy: Jay Naidoo

What exactly is "food security"? The World Food Summit, Rome 1996, defined it as: "Food security exists when all people, at all times, have physical and economic access to sufficient, safe and nutritious food to meet their dietary needs and food preferences for an active and healthy life". While eradicating extreme poverty and hunger became a UN Millennium Development Goal to be eradicated by 2015, a few years short of that goal saw droughts and increased food prices which plunged nearly a billion people into hunger.

The majority of people living with food insecurity are in Africa, and the political tenuousness of many countries fuels the inability to provide food to their populations, and with nearly three-quarters of Africa's entire population living in rural areas, this is of deep concern. While small-scale producers can produce almost 90% of the continent's food, around half of that number remain food insecure. As a result of these numbers, encouraging rural populations to produce their own food, and potentially supply excess to their local communities, becomes a high priority.

"The World Bank has found that a rise in GDP linked to agriculture is around four times more successful in reducing poverty than GDP growth in other sectors of the economy." *World Bank, The Growth Report: Strategies for Sustained Growth and Inclusive Development. Washington, DC: Commission on Growth and Development, World Bank, 2008.*

"The fact that under nutrition, micronutrient deficiency, and over nutrition – the three components of malnutrition – are all poverty driven, means that malnutrition is logically important to Africa, where poverty levels remain the highest in the world. As discussed, child nutrition is of particular concern, with as many as 42% of children in sub-Saharan Africa suffering from stunted growth due to malnutrition. With

Malutis, Free State, South Africa

Photo: Leigh Barrett

more than 200 million people aged 15–24 years on the continent, this is clearly an issue of primary concern to the continent." *SAAIA, A Critical Assessment of the G-20 Food Security Agenda, by Cerkia Bramley*

One of the primary ways to decrease food insecurity is through land tenure: the ability of rural populations to access land ownership, title rights, invest in equipment and labor, as well as securing indirect rights to sell produce, and earn an income that allows people to purchase food. Security also means access to clean water, social and political resources, and labor rights.

Women are finally, slowly, being recognized for the invaluable asset they are in agriculture. With over 400 million women globally involved in working the land, it's shocking that many do not have the right to own the land they farm. According to a report by USAID, women comprise 43% of the agricultural labor force in developing countries, but own less than 10% of the land. Even in countries that protect women's rights constitutionally, inheritance laws and customs often forbid

them from inheriting the land. In those countries, women are less likely to attend school, so literacy rates are low – enabling the further abuse of their rights.

"Research has shown that when women manage household resources, including land, they are more likely to spend money on their children's nutritional needs, education, and health. They are also more likely to engage in climate smart agriculture and to implement practices that increase the household's resilience to climate shocks and climate change." *Women, Land, and Food: The Critical Nexus, Agrilinks.org. MAR 16, 2016*

CASE: SOUTH AFRICA

As the country's middle class expands the further one gets from the days of apartheid, people's diets also become more diverse and the former staple grain diet has shifted to including more poultry and vegetables. And yet, while the country has the potential to feed itself, between 12 and 14 million South Africans go without food every day.

Recently, President Zuma called for a "land ceiling of 12 000 hectares on agricultural land" to redistribute farm land to smaller farmers. While that was a considerable pander to those wanting a form of land redistribution ala Zimbabwe, the call was met with clear derision from those who actually understand the agricultural sector. Farm sizes vary from province to province, and between crop or livestock requirements. Gauteng farms can average less than 500ha, while in the Northern Cape, the average is closer to 5,000ha. SA is climate-sensitive with only 12% land suitable for rain-fed crops. 3% of the land is considered fertile, and 69% can accommodate cattle and sheep grazing in the more arid regions. All this makes smart land management even more imperative.

But, lost in the discussion of redistribution of land are the millions who live in rural areas, many of whom eke out a living on commercial farms. The "old ways" occasionally clash with the new: laborers, newly certain of their rights and determined to improve their lives, battle farmers who are faced with not fully understanding how to deal with a new South Africa. Many of these disputes appear to come down to one simple thing: allowing the workers to create a place where they can establish a secure future.

On my road trip across South Africa earlier this year, I detoured far off my planned route and found myself heading towards Rustler's Valley Farm in the eastern Free State. Once, the venue of an annual multi-day music festival, the farm now belongs to the trustees of the non-profit, EarthRise Trust, which includes former Mandela cabinet minister and Chairman of GAIN

(Global Alliance for Improved Nutrition), Jay Naidoo, who cut his political teeth as General-Secretary of the country's largest federation of trade unions, COSATU, during the years leading to apartheid's demise.

Long passionate about labor rights and food security, the chance to make a difference in a community far from anywhere was not to be missed. Jay Naidoo says the goal of Earthrise Trust "is to grow sustainable local communities, growing healthy food through eco-friendly practices that respect our environment, so that communities can feed themselves, raise their incomes by selling their surpluses in the market and investing in building the homes of their dreams, educating their children and promoting good nutrition and health in a village of the 21st century."

The approximately 170 people who live at Naledi Village and the neighboring Franshoek Village have formed a unique partnership, creating a model of community-driven agricultural entrepreneurship.

The village housing, like so many in rural areas that supply labor to commercial farmers, has a feel of temporariness to it with rundown housing or shacks, held together with odd materials, and the ubiquitous rocks securing the roofs. The insecurity that comes from not knowing from one day to the next if the farmer will evict you, whether through imagined or real trespass, creates a mindset that filters down the generations and there appears little on the horizon but to secure the next day's food and shelter.

Named for the cattle rustlers that would hide their bounty within the sandstone folds of the magnificent Maluti Mountains, Rustlers Valley Farm with its rich

Photo courtesy: Jay Naidoo

Photo courtesy: Jay Naidoo

soil, temperate climate and abundant summer rainfall, accommodated fruit and vegetables on less than half of the 273ha, leaving around one third of the land for cattle and sheep ranching. The occasional serious drought made tourism a viable economic alternative, and for many years the farm played host to a 3-day music festival, where tents supplemented the buildings and lodge, and the conservative neighbors were duly shocked by the near-naked hippies congregating there, some of whom stayed to work their passage until the farm's owner sold up and left, and the music was heard no more.

And that left the villagers again dependent on their employment by local farmers, and trying to survive on largely unskilled labor.

In the years the villagers had worked Rustlers Valley farm, they had built a primary school, provided themselves with water connections, and built a reservoir. Their entrepreneurial efforts extended to developing small household gardens, and earning money from grazing land to maintain the farm.

When EarthRise Trust bought the farm in 2013, one of their first actions was to sign over 42 hectares to the villagers. For the first time, residents were not under constant threat of eviction. Finally able to create their own enterprise, they were now able to support themselves, rather than rely on selling their labor to commercial farmers. Using permaculture techniques, the villagers are now also supplying organic produce to the nearby towns, boosting their income further.

A series of meetings with the villagers took place to find out what the community needed. The answer was profoundly indicative of the priorities of the community: a

Photo courtesy: Jay Naidoo

new school. The current school accommodates about one third of the Naledi village population, from crèche to Grade Six, and the burden is placed on one dedicated teacher who is paid less than one would for a trip to your local mechanic. And yet, without access to supplies or assistance, she devotes her life to getting the kids ready to compete in a fast-changing world.

The recent completion of their first building, constructed entirely by a team in the village, is a new crèche for the children and can be used as a multi-purpose facility for community meetings in the evenings and on the weekends, with a provision for a computer training facility once they can secure a partner and donor. It is the first insulated building, an important consideration when coping with the freezing winters high in the Maluti Mountains.

Naidoo emphasizes how this same plan could work elsewhere: could a famer with a 500ha farm be encouraged to give up a small percentage of the land to the farm workers? Would that small parcel of land be considered a hardship to the landowner, and what impact would it have on labor disputes, where poverty makes petty crime a serious offence, often punished by the eviction of the family – and in some cases, punishment of the entire community by cutting off services to their ramshackle homes?

In light of the socio-economic plan championed by Mandela, called the Reconstruction and Development Program (RDP), aimed at trying to catch up on the backlog of housing and services for those who struggled with poverty during apartheid, and which remains too slow on delivery

Photo courtesy: Jay Naidoo

for residents, sometimes taking 5 years to complete a house, Naidoo says, "Imagine if each of us could do something small to deliver on the RDP program? I look around and see how land lies idle in the hands of absentee landlords while huge shanty towns surround even rural towns. We could have insisted, just like in Naledi Village, that land be shared with farmworkers, who could be mentored by the farmers to become entrepreneurs and benefit from the food value chain, including access to the market.…We would by today have created millions of community-driven livelihoods in agriculture, secured household food security, eliminated malnutrition and made a huge dent in poverty. I know that there is nothing in our Constitution that stops us from achieving this goal."

It's a common problem in rural communities – largely overlooked or forgotten by politicians, and undervalued by farmers who depend on them for production, but who believe they're simply replaceable because of their arguable lack of skills. There is also the issue of changing and modernizing labor practices – it's sometimes hard for farmers who, for generations, have farmed a certain way, and been allowed to treat their labor without recourse, to fully understand a new South Africa and the rights workers now have. All that, combined with politicians who are mostly left alone to rule their municipality like fiefdoms, and it becomes clear that money talks, labor walks.

In 2015, residents of the nearby town of Ficksburg marched angrily to the Municipal Offices in protest of the City Council's corruption. Accused of theft, fraud, cronyism, and a failure to deliver much-needed services resulted in an inquiry which re-

Photo courtesy: Jay Naidoo

vealed a municipality in complete disarray. With a population of just over 125,000 people in 22.5 square miles, it is an extremely important area in terms of agriculture and tourism, considered the "gateway to Lesotho". While the inquiry continues, town and rural residents seem determined to see an end to the bucket toilets, sewer spillages, and inaccessibility to potable water that have been a part of their struggle for generations.

With a group like EarthRise Trust leading by example, perhaps there is a way through the issues of land tenure and food insecurity that doesn't require government intervention, but can encourage existing land owners and farmers to look at this problem in a new way. President Zuma may talk of land redistribution in unrealistic, Zimbabwe-like terms, but there might just be a way that Africans can deal with their problems, without being forced to do so.

"We will eradicate hunger, build social cohesion, empower women, improve nutrition, health and education. But most importantly we would be delivering on our promise in 1994 of a 'better life for all'. And that is priceless." – *Jay Naidoo*

CALL FOR CONTENT

Perspective Publications is now accepting content for the December 2016 issue of **PERSPECTIVE: AFRICA.**

We welcome editorials, op-eds, policy discussions, essays, photojournalism, art, satire, cultural reviews, and more.

We encourage well-presented, deeply researched material on a diverse range of topics that reflect the region concerned.

Submissions guidelines are available to view on the website:
http://perspective-publications.com

Perspective Publications is available in digital and print editions on all international **Amazon.com** sites.

Selected articles can be found on the website.

Individual stories and photo essays may be ordered directly from Perspective Publications.

In the Public Eye

By Mandy Tomson

THE DENIERS

Imagine what it must be like to know that your obstinate illogic caused the deaths of hundreds of thousands of people? What a horrendous burden to bear. Don't ask Tony Blair, George W. Bush or Thabo Mbeki. They simply will not take responsibility for the hundreds of thousands of unnecessary deaths caused by their irrationality, despite mountains of evidence that forever condemns them as the 21st century's first mass murderers. Iraq was destroyed and the South African funeral industry flourished. And yet Bush hides out in Texas, Blair rambles defensively and incoherently, and Mbeki still rants on about drug companies and apparently feels that a high death rate would be preferable to any sort of profit for the pharmaceutical industry.

Robert MacFarlane, US Secretary of Defence during the Vietnam War, is the only example I can recall in modern history of a man who actually took responsibility and analysed his mistakes and moral responsibility for the US's catastrophic involvement in Vietnam. That took guts but at least the man had a conscience he felt the need to clear. What was most impressive about his apology and analysis is that he wasn't even on trial! After all, it's self-serving to express regret and remorse (on the advice of your attorney) when you know you are facing prison.

Inkaaaaandla…! The not so final chapter

Even though Jacob Zuma makes decent money, there is no way he has R7 million in savings for which he can legitimately account and on which he has paid taxes. I have no doubt that he has a great deal of money in his charitable trusts but he has not filed proper paperwork and paying for Nkandla out of this money would raise more questions. He could receive "donations" to use to repay the money but he would have to pay donations tax and questions would arise as to who is donating and why. Plus, no one is keen to donate to a lame-duck president whose ability to deliver financial rewards to his cronies is waning. Zuma is in a chilli pickle. Finally, our nation's venerable, determined investigative journalists will begin following the money which is key to understanding what has been going on under Zuma's presidency.

EDUCATION

Another half year has passed and there has been no structural improvement or change in South Africa's education system for millions of children, meaning our annual poor matric results and related recriminations will arrive in January 2017 – as predictable as the sun rising in the east.

If I adopt a dog, the SPCA will inspect my home to make sure I have a fenced garden and will interrogate me to make sure I appear to have the appropriate temperament to qualify as a suitable dog owner. However, humankind doesn't issue licenses for parenting. Whether from a wealthy or poor family in any country on earth, children have no guarantee that they will be brought into the world by emotionally balanced, dedicated parents; they have no assurance that a rich mom and dad won't destroy their self-esteem by palming them off onto nannies and technology, and no guarantee that a poor, teenage parent won't lock them up at home and go off to party on weekends. The circumstances of our births are a crapshoot and there are millions of abandoned children in every country on earth that confirm that not every adult makes a suitable parent.

This is precisely why education is so important – it is meant to be the great equaliser in any society. No matter what type of background you have, you should have the opportunity to go to a decent school with a solid academic program and basic arts and sports facilities where you are exposed to decent, caring adults who can give you the care, guidance and inspiration that may be lacking at home. South Africa lacks this basic insurance that gives children from all walks of life a shot at happiness and a decent future. Many successful people from dysfunctional family backgrounds have credited one teacher for helping them to see the light and triumph over personal adversity. Tragically, our bankrupt basic ed-

ucation system eliminates the only avenue that some children have to express their potential.

Education is the major failure of the South African government (and many others). The frustrating thing is that it isn't rocket science. Millions of children are caged by an inept, passive government and a militant, disgustingly selfish teachers union, the South African Democratic Teachers Union, which is hell-bent on the unconditional protection of dubious teachers who beat and sexually abuse their students, or simply don't show up. And yet those fortunate enough to actually make it to university against all odds want government resources devoted to an entirely free education and appear to have forgotten the primary and high schools from which they just emerged.

MARIJUANA

When is any African country going to legalise marijuana? I am nauseated by all this social conservatism when marijuana is an ancient, natural remedy. Even the Afrikaners used to drink dagga tea, and marijuana was only declared illegal in the 1930s.

Africa is always behind the curve and it is exhausting and depressing. Even the pleas of the late Inkatha Freedom Party member of parliament, Mario Oriano-Ambrosini, did not move any South African political party to propose a marijuana legalisation bill.

Every year, untold millions are wasted chasing, prosecuting and imprisoning people for possession of and dealing in marijuana in a country where two-thirds of murders remain unsolved. The benefits of marijuana are medically indisputable and of particular import in a country with a high rate of HIV/AIDS where people could really benefit from a natural anti-anxiety and appetite-stimulating herb. The staid, old, white ladies who volunteer at frail-care facilities on the South Coast are forced to approach any man with dreadlocks to ask for marijuana oil so they can distribute it to the elderly. It's ridiculous.

Um, excuse me, President Mbeki: given your obsessive resistance to the pharmaceutical treatment of HIV/AIDS and your preference for home-grown remedies, why have you not actually done something useful by spearheading the struggle to legalise marijuana?

To submit content for this regular column, please contact The Editor at editor@perspective-publications.org

Essays, artwork, satire welcome.

ABOUT

PERSPECTIVE PUBLICATIONS

The world is getting smaller, and the more we understand it, the better we, and future generations, will be equipped to deal with its complexities.

LOOKING AT THE WORLD THROUGH A

HUMANITARIAN LENS

Perspective Publications is a South African-based independent, multimedia endeavor, with print and digital editions, as well as a website and blog.

http://perspective-publications.com

Africa By The Maps

Colonial Africa, on the eve of World War 1

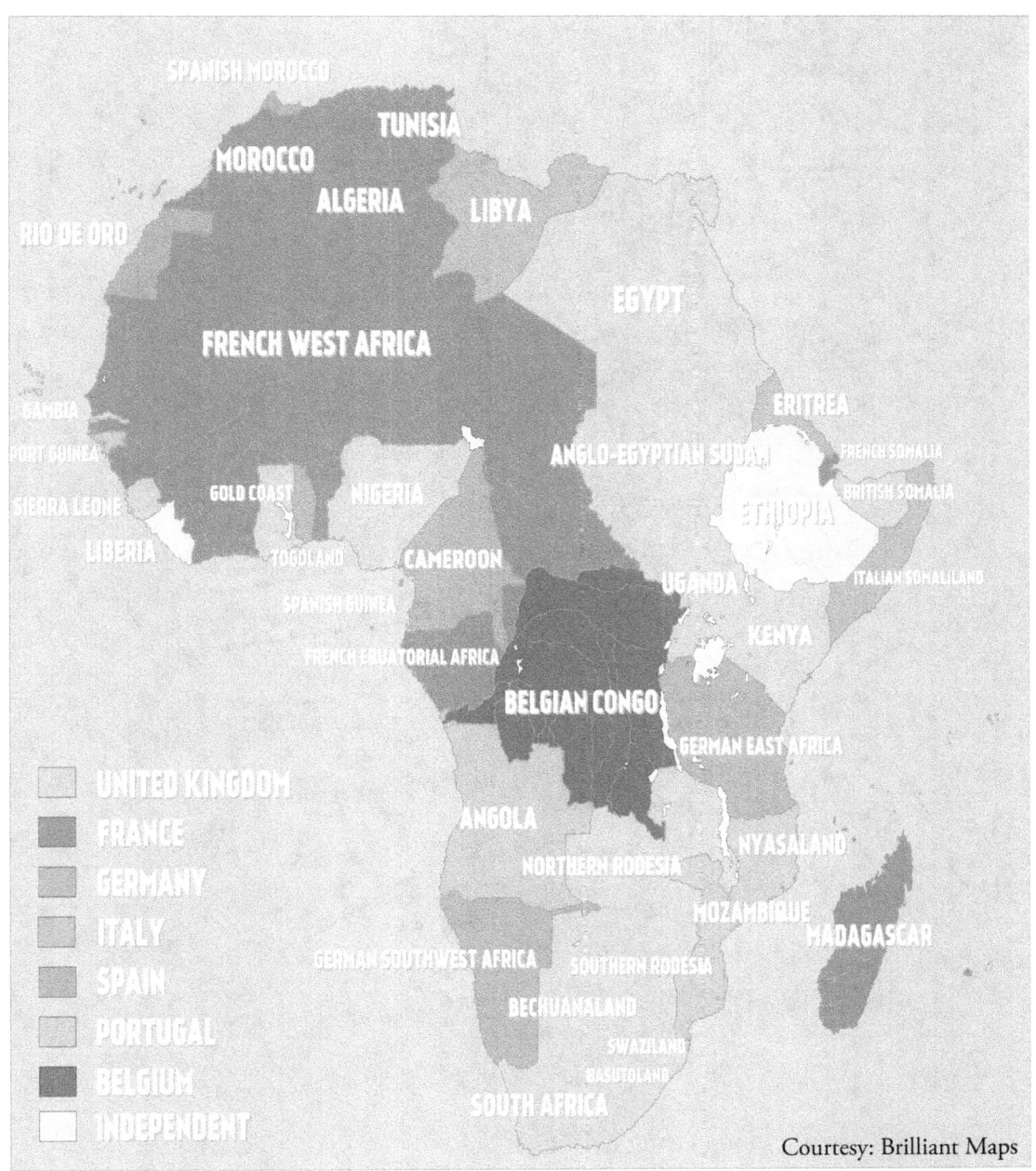

Courtesy: Brilliant Maps

A World In One Continent

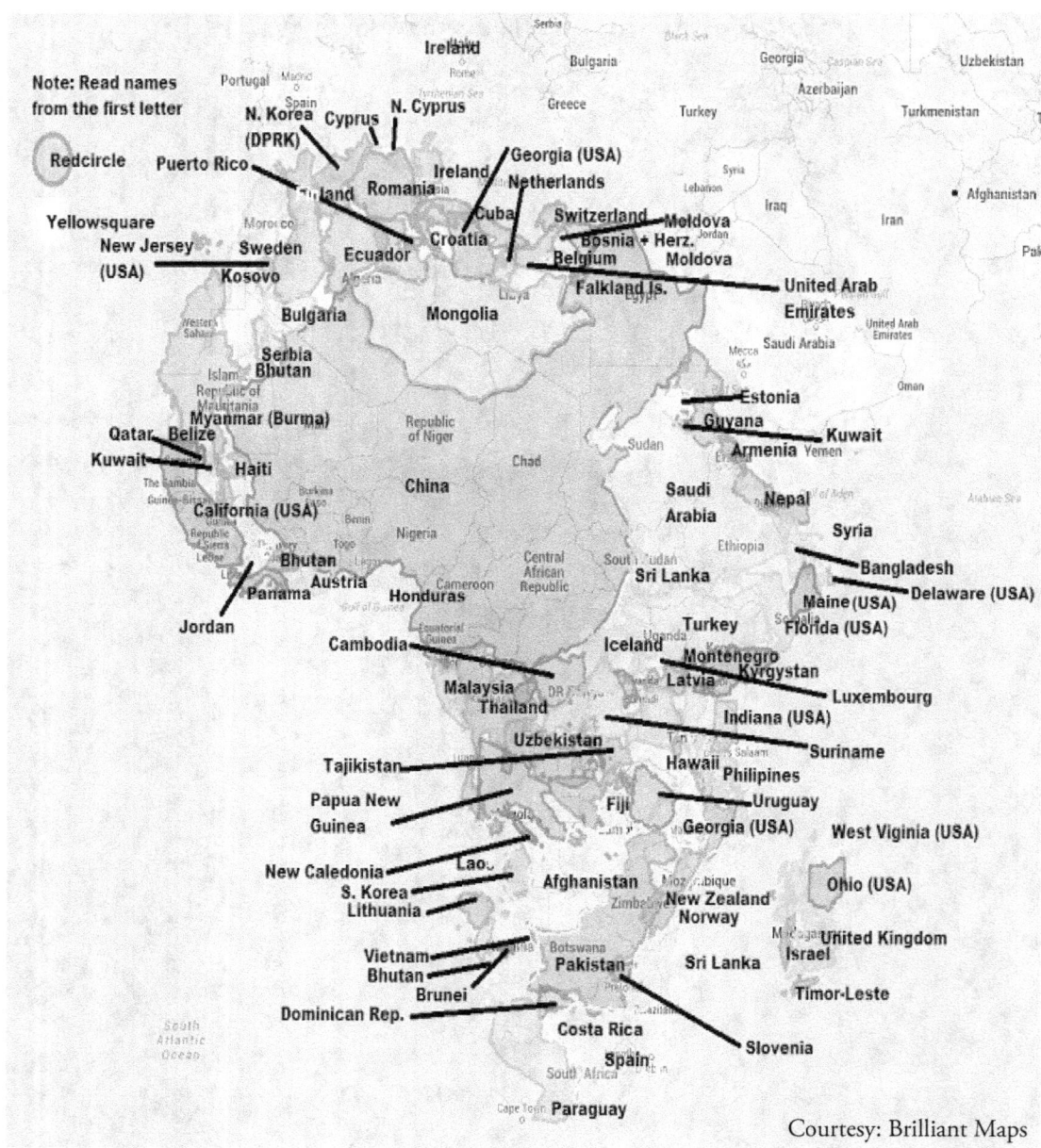

Courtesy: Brilliant Maps

Missionary Willem Janszoon Blaeu's 17th Century map of Africa. Illustrations of Africa were added to unexplored areas.

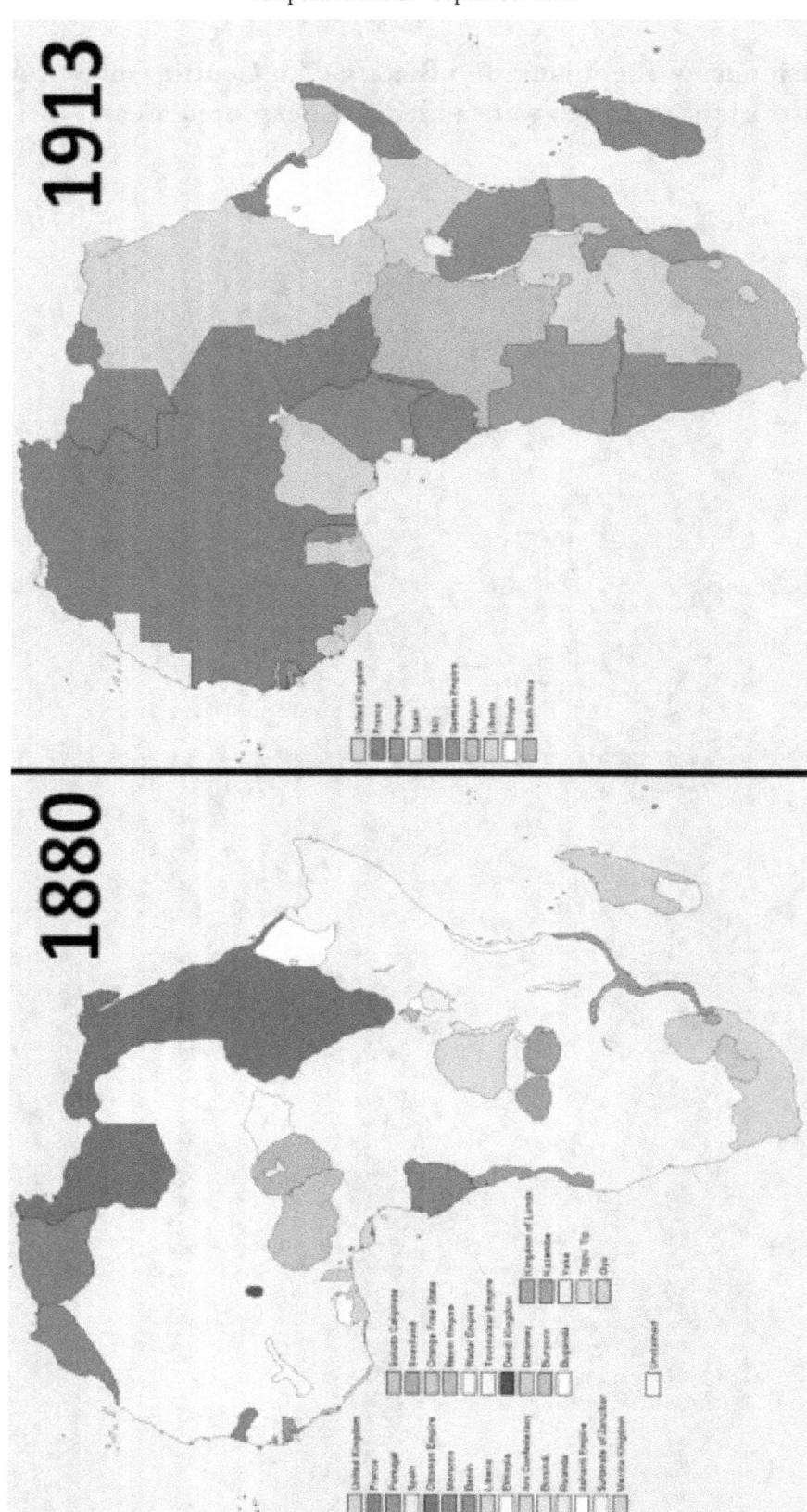

A European missionary's map of Africa, circa 1908

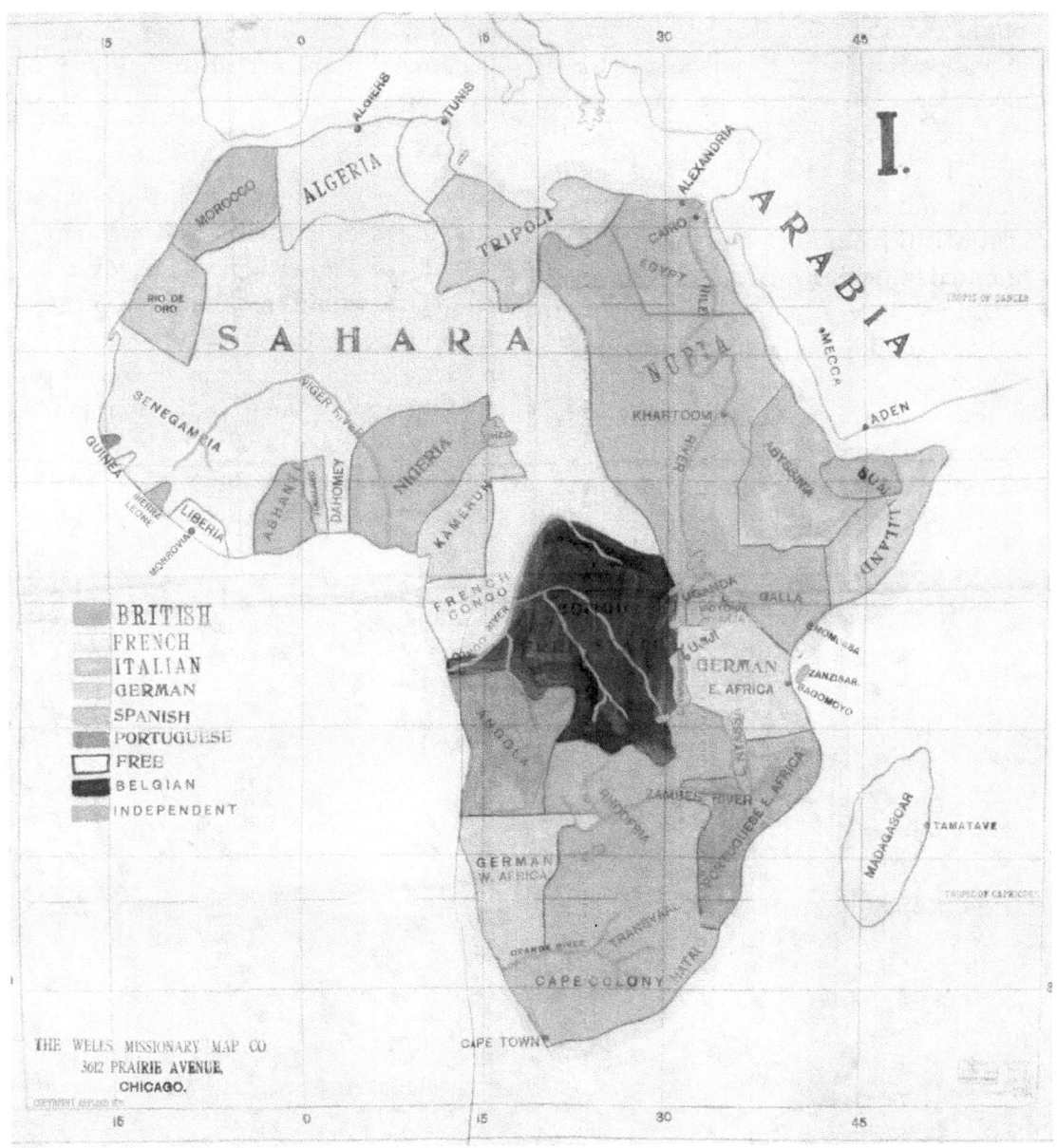

Mediators Beyond Borders International- Investing in Peace

by Anna Milovanovic, MBBI, USA

For the last ten years, Mediators Beyond Borders International (MBBI), has promoted peacebuilding by advocating for mediation at all levels. Currently working in: Colombia, Cambodia, Kenya, Nepal, Sierra Leone, Uganda, Greece and South Sudan; and elsewhere for previous projects, MBBI has trained more than twelve hundred individuals. Local partners invite MBBI volunteer teams of mediators and peacebuilders to jointly design and implement projects that increase local abilities to heal from violent conflict; reconcile torn communities; and prevent, manage, and transform conflict. Additionally, MBB Consulting, a division of MBBI, was created to advance business interests, community needs, government accountability and socially responsible development.

Kenya

Easy access to weapons, arbitrary boundaries, water scarcity, mismanagement of natural resources and grazing have escalated violence within traditional pastoralist communities in Kenya. MBBI's Kenya Initiative (members pictured below) supports the application of indigenous peacebuilding processes in these communities, working with local partners to build an extensive network of local peace guard-

MBBI's Kenyan Initiative
Photo courtesy MBBI

ians who are thus empowered to resolve their own conflicts and build sustainable peace.

The impacted communities, after implementing alternative dispute resolution models, are able to see the following successes: the number of conflict-related deaths has been almost zero; communities help return lost or stolen livestock to other communities; weekly inter-ethnic peace committee meetings with women, elders and youth, discuss issues and largely use restorative justice processes to keep the peace and manage criminal activities. Further, children have been able to return to school and new schools have been built; economic activity has increased; and peace guardians respond to early signs of conflict on their way to becoming peacebuilders for surrounding communities. **This is positive peace**—where relationships are restored, social and economic systems serve the entire inter-ethnic community, and there is constructive resolution of conflict.

South Sudan

MBBI has also worked in South Sudan, where generations of South Sudanese have experienced waves of violence. More than two million citizens are displaced, almost half the country faces food insecurity and some children have been recruited as child soldiers. The United Nations Special Envoy on Sexual Violence says this is the worst sexual violence she has ever seen. MBBI's South Sudan team recognizes that trauma plays a role in continuing the cycle of violence: that hurting people hurt people. With that in mind, MBBI's team of clinicians and

peacebuilders has sought to increase resilience against incitement to fight, particularly among the new generation of South Sudanese youth.

MBBI, with local and international partners, focused efforts in Protection of Civilians (POC) camps, which shelter tens of thousands of internally displaced people, as well as in two of the most deeply affected areas near the capital city of Juba. The project trained South Sudanese women, youth, and civil society on understanding trauma and practical, day-to-day support that promotes healing. Participants in the trainings learned of the relationship between trauma and risk of violence, and gained tools needed to resolve conflict nonviolently.

When the POC camps close and people return to their homes, there is potential for conflict between returnees and those living in their communities. By working with the South Sudanese in both the POC camps and in the greater-Juba area, MBBI South Sudan prepares these communities for reconciliation. When the situation is safe for the MBBI team to return, the project will continue with its trauma-informed peacebuilding approach to begin to heal the psychological wounds afflicting the young nation.

Sierra Leone

In Sierra Leone, MBBI engaged local grassroots activists (pictured) in dialogue about their future—empowering them to promote a peaceful election in 2012.

The activists feared that violence might destroy the country's fragile peace, so university students grew the coalition into a movement of 40 organizations. Then,

Building Unity for Peaceful Elections in Sierra Leone: A Dialogue and Conflict Transformation Skills Workshop, was set up for diverse stakeholder groups throughout the nation. This provided 250 stakeholders with the knowledge and skills to advance peaceful elections. There were no incidents of violence during Sierra Leone's third general election since its civil war ended.

Although the Ebola crisis in 2014 imposed travel restrictions and prevented in-person trainings, the team continued their work by using an online platform. MBBI conducted a Training of Trainers program in conflict transformation. The trainings provided the leaders with skills to work with conflict and trauma resulting from the Ebola crisis. These leaders will now play a crucial role in mitigating epidemic related conflicts. Additionally, MBBI and its local partners aspire to create a peacebuilding institute with pro-

grams on: youth leadership and empowerment, women's leadership empowerment, mediation training for tribal chiefs, and conflict transformation for training of trainers.

Liberia

MBBI's Liberia Initiative ran from 2007-2012, and supported the establishment of a mediation service for Liberian refugees in the Buduburam refugee camp. The initiative enhanced the capacity for mediation among a wide range of Ghanaian officials and Liberian civil society; facilitated the safe re-integration of 75 ex-combatants into their communities following vocational training and psychosocial support; and brought together women of nine tribes to reweave the social fabric in their fractured society. Previous projects have informed the work of MBBI's goal of local capacity building for sustained peace and community em-

MBBI's Sierra Leone Initiative
Photo courtesy MBBI

powerment, while providing MBBI with strong foundational support.

MBBI in Africa

What's next for MBBI in Africa? Its budding **Uganda** project team is poised to work on issues of land rights and denationalization of property. Uganda's population is growing and conflict arises inter-generationally as land resources in the agrarian state become increasingly scarce. Thus, MBBI will begin mediation in areas of need identified by local partners and concerned parties.

MBBI is structured around project teams, regional and working groups. Its United Nations and Rotary International Working Groups are building bridges and endeavoring to strengthen the peace work of these two important international organizations. MBBI is looking to expand its regional groups to Southern and West Africa, following on successful models in Canada and the United Kingdom. Regional Groups create a space for open dialogue among MBBI members of a certain geographical region, to engage with each other and facilitate projects on

the ground.

If you are interested in building sustainable peace and resilient communities, learn how you can get involved at the below website or donate to one of our African country projects. Your generous gift helps MBBI continue its work, answering the call of local partners seeking expertise and guidance in dealing with: conflict, overcoming trauma and restoring relationships, supporting mediation programs, and most importantly, building a more peace "able" world.

http://mediatorsbeyondborders.org/

MBB is a tax-exempt, 501(c)3,
not-for-profit organization.

An Extraordinary Life, Lived Ordinarily

by Leigh Barrett

It was her laugh that caught me. The clear, joyous, uninhibited peel rung out unexpectedly, belying her life of odds stacked against odds. A 21-year old woman, studying to pass matric so she can enter nursing school she can't afford in an effort to make life better for her, her family, and her 2-year old son, living financially insecure in a home too small for the 8 people her police constable mother now supports on a single salary in Mfuleni Township, a relic of apartheid and an obstacle to advancement, too far from anywhere to realistically find employment or accessibility to a better life.

And she's HIV positive. With Tuberculosis.

In a country – and a world – more than capable of dealing a death blow to HIV transmission, but lacking the political will to do so Anathi* contracted HIV as a teenager, nursing an uncle and his children who were HIV positive, without the benefit of training or knowledge beyond very basic hygiene.

She tells me, "I felt afraid because I wanted to know where I got it. I didn't sleep with a boyfriend. I found out in 2010, when I was 15. I was shocked and didn't feel comfortable, so I only went to the clinic in 2011 and got the treatment. Now, I feel happy – I don't have stress that someone will see me there. I don't care about others, I care about my life."

Photo: Leigh Barrett

Anathi and photojournalist, Paul Ratje, walking to the Ivan Toms Clinic. Mfuleni, Cape Town

Preparing sheep heads for sale to passers-by. Mfuleni, Cape Town

Photo: Leigh Barrett

And yet, Anathi still insisted on anonymity for this piece, because very few people know she has HIV. The stigma, prejudice, and discrimination that accompanies having the disease is still prevalent. When she discovered that she was HIV positive, the family's reaction was to evict her from the home, a situation now reversed, but Anathi's mother still struggles to overcome her prejudice. With roughly one in eight people living with HIV, the real life consequences can range from a denial of care to a loss of employment, and depression or a sense of worthlessness.

Undermining people with HIV has a dire impact on the spread of the disease: refusing care, whether it's from professionals or the community, creates a sense of shame that pushes the person into denial. And that is the most dangerous place to be: South Africa alone is seeing over 300,000 new cases each year, with around 200,000 South Africans dying from AIDS-related diseases. 48% of the 7 million people living with HIV are on antiretroviral treat-

Photo: Leigh Barrett

ments.

By comparison, USA, with 1,2 million HIV-positive people (less than 40% on antiretroviral treatment) is seeing close to 50,000 new HIV cases each year, and the UK around 6,000 new cases, adding to nearly 104,000 people with HIV, 91% of whom are on antiretrovirals. *(Source: Avert. org)*

The stigma attaches itself for a variety of reasons. There is an irrational response to those who have HIV, with still too many viewing them as promiscuous, or homosexual, or with a lifestyle that doesn't fit the adopted "biblical" ideal.

For many years, HIV was automatically associated with death. AIDS was the logical conclusion to being HIV positive, and nobody recovered. With the advancement and accessibility of drugs, that is no longer

the case, and while infected people are able to live long and relatively healthy lives, they still face that fear. Denial and secrecy remain the chosen course for the afflicted, undermining the ability to stop the transmission of the disease.

When someone famous says something that is a fundamental, known, truth, it gets headlines, and that was the case when Charlize Theron, speaking at the 21st International Aids Conference, said, "I think it's time we face the truth about the unjust world we live in…. We have every tool we need to prevent the spread of HIV….The real reason we haven't beaten the epidemic boils down to one simple fact: We value some lives more than others."

In the 1980's, when the world started to learn about HIV and AIDS and it was still considered a "gay disease", Health Ministers from numerous African countries

Photo: Leigh Barrett

absolutely denied even the existence of homosexuality in their country, and that negative message drove gay relationships, as well as prostitution, into the shadows, resulting in an epidemic.

In 2016, while some countries have slowly come around to reality, there is still a resistance to the acknowledgment of homosexual behavior (despite it being quite acceptable prior to the arrival of Christian missionaries on the continent), with still too many countries making human relationships punishable by death.

Healthcare workers, like young Anathi, can be victims or perpetrators. Many in rural areas do not have access to professional care, so do their best for family members stricken with AIDS-related illnesses. Their lack of access to proper hygiene, or simple ignorance about the ways in which HIV can be transmitted, has led to the spreading of the disease. As low as that risk can be, for someone like Anathi, it's hard to explain to people that she is neither promiscuous, a drug user, nor a prostitute.

And, if one cannot trust a professional healthcare worker to keep your status confidential, especially in small communities where everyone knows each other, there is valid reason to keep one's condition secret – or not get tested at all.

In 2014, Anathi discovered she had Tuberculosis. "Why me?" was her first obvious question. "What did I do? And then, I found out that TB is all around. The mothers I was helping at the clinic already had TB, and I didn't know."

Across South Africa, Tuberculosis is the main driver of HIV. An airborne disease, TB affects HIV/AIDS patients, as well as smokers, more often than any other illness. According to the WHO (2011), 13% of all people with TB also have HIV, and with the high HIV rates in sub-Saharan Africa, this is particularly serious. TB is one of the main side effects of poverty: overcrowding, unsanitary conditions, resource-poor communities, with limited access to healthcare - all elements that are commonly found in the townships of South Africa. Co-infection means that regardless of which came first, TB or HIV, each disease encourages the progress of the other.

"We cannot win the battle against AIDS if we do not also fight TB. TB is too often a death sentence for people with AIDS. It does not have to be this way. We have known how to cure TB for more than 50 years. What we have lacked is the will and the resources to quickly diagnose people with TB and get them the treatment they need." Nelson Mandela July 15, 2004.

"Your hair is so clean", she said quietly, as if more to herself than to me. Her talents for hairdressing are one way Anathi makes a little money to provide for the household of dependents. Visiting the local HIV health clinic where she receives, and often provides, counselling there are poems on the walls, written by young residents who are now faced with a lifetime of medication, and their struggle to face down the odds of living in poor conditions, is as daunting to them as it sounds.

In townships with proximity to the larger cities like Cape Town, there are clearly more services provided, more support, and better management of treatment. The rural areas are not quite as fortunate, with access limited to groups providing clinic services. Bhekisisa, the health news arm of the highly regarded Mail & Guardian newspaper, reports from the small town of Eshowe that adherence groups are increasing and having an impact. These groups, or clubs, are for those on treatment and doing well, and are designed to encourage HIV-positive patients to remain on treatment, especially when they feel healthy. The goal is to relieve the pressure on nurses, allowing them to free up time to treat the seriously ill. For patients who are responding well to ART's, and only need to be seen once a year, they can now simply collect medication from a location outside of the clinic. In Anathi's case, feeling healthy led to her skipping medication, and being more at risk of contracting TB.

The light at the end of this very long tunnel appears to be coming in the form of HIV vaccine trials, beginning in November 2016. This is the first time a large-scale clinical trial of such a vaccine will be embarked upon, and appears to show promise in dealing with the strain that dominates in southern Africa.

Not her real name.

Photo: Leigh Barrett

Photo: Paul Ratje

What did I do to you
Why you hate me so much
What do I deserve
To get so much punishment

Even if you hate me
What would you gain
You'll live with it
You'll die with it

Now I am free
I am done crying
Someone told me not to cry
Do you know who is it
An angel

It is so sweet
It is kind
It never deceive me
So I know my destiny

A poem from the wall of the health clinic treating
HIV/Aids patients, Mfuleni Cape Town

Camissa vs Coloured
Challenging Continued 'Race-Labeling'

By Patric Tariq Mellet

Somebody in the Olympic stadium in Rio was overheard correcting someone else who has just shouted "Wayde van Niekerk the black South African has taken gold and smashed the world record for 400 meters. "He's not Black", she said – "he is Coloured".

Across the world people started asking "what on earth are these South Africans talking about when they use the archaic old racist term, 'Coloured folks', which went out of use over 50 years ago - and they say they don't mean that they're 'Black folks' either?"

The recent Constitutional Court finding against the state for practicing discrimination against Coloured employees in the Department of Correctional Services and the astounding achievement of Wayde van Niekerk at the Rio Olympics suddenly gave impetus to an old yet still very passionate debate, underpinned by much pain, as to whether it was appropriate to be still using the colonial and Apartheid race label 'COLOURED' for the range of communities that fell outside of those considered 'White' and, those considered to fall under the peculiar South African ethnicised meaning of 'Black'.

In South Africa after the 1976 youth uprisings, the Apartheid regime got rid of using the rejected term 'Bantu' which had replaced the term 'Native' and dealt the Black Consciousness Movement a deadly blow by using the term 'Black' in a narrow ethnic sense to denote only those tribally identified with predominantly sub-Saharan African roots but excluding those identifying as Khoena, San, Griqua, Nama, Korana and 'Coloured', suggesting that these cannot be regarded as native. It is unfortunate that the ANC has held onto this definition and in fact held onto the 'four-race silo' approach of the Apartheid-era and this has done much to keep racism alive and flourishing in South Africa. It is not because there has been no alternative to the pseudo-scientific notion of 'race' for recognising diversity. South Africans who may self-identify, fall into just three broad families of people all with a strong affinity to Africa – Africans, Afro-Europeans and Afro-Asians. In each of these there is a diversity of sub-community identities shaped by history, experience and heritage. This has nothing to do with race, should have nothing to do with politics and the state should have no business in forcing people into identity silos. This was a cornerstone of Apartheid.

Where people saw themselves in terms of the three streams of overarching heritage, or in the many different community heritages as subsets of these, was a personal and community matter of self-identification. People could express affinities to a number of these at the same time. It is a personal prerogative. In a country where class has always co-related almost absolutely with colour, there should be no need to use the race-lexicon or even community identities as the means for socio-economic redress of the past. Class parameters can easily be used to address affirmation and level the opportunity playing field. Indeed, it can do so in a much more just and focused manner and could have avoided the opportunism and corruption by persons who, simply on the base of race, could stand at the front of the queue for redress over and over again, while the real poor continued in abject poverty and experiencing the colonial experience under a new neo-colonial elite of colour.

Over the last decade, I have done much writing on this subject and, in more recent days, General Jeremy Vearey published a letter on social media and in a Cape Town newspaper on the subject, too. In his letter, he recalled a debate in the ANC journal SECHABA back in the mid-1980s when Alex la Guma, Arnold Selby and I (writing as PG – a member of Sechaba's editorial board) opened a debate on the same subject, which raged on for some time and included contributions from Reg September, Jack Simons, and others. In the course of the debate, we separated out a number of things that were being conflated as one. Namely, the label 'Coloured' as an imposed term of identity, needed to be separated from a number of other pertinent issues.

We said that we needed to interrogate whether there were a set of distinct communities of people who had been herded together under this label and if so, who were they and what may they want in terms of self-identification? Under the Apartheid categorisation, 'Coloured' included six sub-categories – Cape Coloured, Cape Malay, Griqua, Nama, San, and Other Coloured. Initially, Indians and Chinese were also categorised as 'Coloured', but later Eben Donges who was antagonistically obsessed with Indians decided that there should be as separate race classification for Asiatic.

We also needed to ask ourselves, now that this constructed tenuous identity has been around for over more than a century and entrenched, whether it can just be wished away? There are many people who either do not know about this painful past or do not want to know about or do not care what happened to their people before they were born….. they just loved to be known as Coloured (and that may be their right, too). There are yet others who say – "to hell with any type of name or identity – I don't need identities… I am a human and a free-thinker and don't want to be boxed in any way. Let me be." That is a legitimate choice, too.

Importantly, we all felt incensed that both the Apartheid regime and many in the ANC referred to Coloured people as a 'non-African' minority and both also discriminated against Coloured people. We also felt incensed that

the unity of people of colour who had collectively used the term 'Black' in a unitary fashion under the Black Consciousness Movement was undermined by both the Apartheid regime and some within the ANC who embraced the term 'Black' and gave it a narrow ethnicised meaning – namely referring only to descendants of sub-Saharan Africans who had predominantly Bantu ethnicity falling under a specific basket of tribes. This excluded and marginalised Cape Khoena, San, Nama, Griqua and those broadly called Coloured. Many of us felt that the embracing of the ANC of the ethnicised meaning of Black and equally an ethnicised ownership of 'African' was contrary to the first constitution of the ANC drafted in 1919, and Prof Jack Simons, senior ANC political commissar, pointed this out in the 1980s. That constitution said that anyone with at least one forebear who was indigenous to Africa was an African in terms of membership criteria.

More importantly, even with all of these questions we raised, and those of us alive still raise, is the fact that as much as the amaXhosa, Zulu, BaSotho, Shangaan, Venda, BaTswana et al exist as Africans and as part of the diverse South African family of communities, so do those unfairly herded under the label 'coloured' – Griqua, San, Korana, Nama and various surviving Cape Khoena communities. Also, there are those who do not neatly fall into these groups but have ancestral genealogical and DNA connections to all of these, but also to slaves brought from West and East Africa, India and Southeast Asia, as well as some European and other migrant ancestry. It is this latter group that has struggled with expressing their sub-identity as South African. Do they create some kind of revivalist affinity identity as 'KhoiSan' (also a questionable anthropological term) or do they knock on one or another door of the marginalised survivalist Khoena formations, make common cause and ask to be let in? Taking those options would require that they engage in denial of their Bantu slave and indentured labour roots, their Indian and Southeast Asian slave roots, and even their

European roots. So is there really any option but to embrace the 'Coloured' label?

These are all vexing questions. Some posit that "why can we not just bury all of these sub- identities – wish them away and simply all just be South Africans? Others say why can't we just bury all of these community and cultural identities and just be Africans? Others say, "I just want to be Black; we people of colour should stand united as 'Black' South Africans - meaning all people of colour as we share a common black experience!" Others want to walk over the rights of South Africans of perceived predominantly Bantu heritage and make false claims that 'Coloured' people are the only true descendants of the Khoena and San when everyone knows that almost every tribal group in South Africa has Khoena and San ancestry to one degree or another and we also know that up to half of those who were classified as 'Coloured' in part have Bantu

linages, too. The proper terminology in fact is Sub-Saharan Ancestry and Southern African Ancestry, the latter being the forebears of the Khoena and San, but also of other identifiable groups right up to Tanzania and Angola. Then there are those who simply hold racist views and hate the people they call 'Blacks' and emphasise that they consider 'Coloured' not to be black but brown. (bruin). This dates back to a specific propaganda campaign of PW Botha to promote the concept of 'bruine-Afrikaner' to rural Coloured townships. We all know that that the 'bruin' concept is nonsense, because those labeled 'Coloured' range in tones from the whitest white to the blackest black.... but some buy into this and love it. During the 1994 election, a TV camera captured an interview with Coloured gentleman who introduced himself as Kaffertjie Swart, and was in skintone the deepest black in colour. He called himself a bruin-ou ("brown man") and

Kaapse Klopse (Minstrel Parade)

Photo Clarissa De Wet 2009

proceeded to tell the world that he was going to vote for de Klerk because he did not want a "black kaffir" living next door to him. There are, unfortunately for good discourse, plenty of falsehoods that abound.

When more thought is applied to these expressions, none of these stand up to scrutiny as progressive approaches on what some call the "Coloured Question".

Colonialism and imperialism battered African communities and tried to panel-beat people into imperialist-determined borders and oneness. Community identities and cultures were repressed in the name of civilisation and as part of the peace agreed by two colonial factions – Boer and British - when South Africa was created just over 100 years ago. The British largely decided who in Southern Africa was to be in South Africa and who was to be left out and for much of the 20th century, people of colour had no rights in South Africa. Under these circumstances, it would be a travesty of justice to accede to just being South African, whatever that may mean. Besides the injustice to the diverse communities inside the South Africa borders, what of the Southern Africans outside of these borders who were a huge part of building the South Africa economic powerhouse. Bury community cultural identities? God forbid…Why? This was what colonialism tried to do all of these years.

Now here is the biggest issue. Should a cultural, spiritual, social, economic, political historical experience and heritage of a people, called Coloured, who first emerged as a creole formation over 400 years ago simply be set aside for political expediency? Over the years these people were given many different names.… Afrikanders and Free Blacks were just two of the names previously used.

When Asian and European ships started frequently visiting Cape shores from the early 15th century it left impacts on indigene communities, as happened all over the world where different cultures engaged. These, however, were not dramatic. But in the 17th century when 1,071 ships called at Table Bay in the first 50 years and another 1,600 by the end of the century, dramatic changes occurred. The indigenes initially met the challenges posed by establishing fairly complex port relations – stevedoring, trading, having representatives travel abroad, and effectively establishing a port with a proto-settlement at the Camissa River flowing from Table Mountain to the sea. In 1652, however, there was effectively a hostile takeover of the port business and settlement of the Goringhaicona at Camissa by the Dutch VOC under the command of Jan van Riebeeck - and this changed the trajectory of our history.

In that period of 1600 – 1652, the indigene population came into contact with Europeans, and most likely with Asians and other Africans, in large numbers when soldiers, sailors and others stopped over for lengthy stays at the Cape. As in any port all over the world, various types of sexual encounters would have taken place and children were born of these. Recorded accounts note that some in the local community looked very similar to Europeans but were not. When thousands upon thousands of slaves were brought to the Cape from other parts of Africa, and from India and Southeast Asia, and when Europeans married indigenes and slaves, children were also born. Slaves were the largest population group for over a century after the Khoena were forced out of the Western Cape, other than those Khoena forced into servitude and conscripted into commandos. This history cannot be wished away.

But this is not the only aspect of what can be called the Camissa Footprint or experience. Camissa represents the genesis of heritage involving loss of life, land, liberty and identity and the resistance struggles manifested in rising above adversity. It incorporated the embrace between those struggling with enslavement and those struggling with dispossession of the port settlement and their livelihood, forced removal, livestock theft, land dispossession and conquest by the might of the gun and even genocide. The San suffered near obliteration in comparison to the Khoena and because of the tendency to overlay San history and heritage with the Khoena story or skewed Khoisan revivalism we continue to mete out injustice to San or /Xam heritage. The mutual embrace of Slave-Indigenes forebears with some of the rebel and non-conformists among the Europeans is also too often written out of our scripts by both whites and people of colour.

The Camissa port community is representative of a unique human coming together through struggles to overcome adversity in the face of the oppressive might of first the Dutch VOC and then the British and then the Union and Apartheid order of white nationalism and Apartheid. As much as the Camissa port settlement started by the Goringhaicona was driven underground, and as much as the very river was driven underground, so too has its descendant's identity based on this heritage been overlaid by layer upon layer of camouflage.

The label 'Coloured' and the ridiculous Apartheid definition thereof has robbed people of their heritage rooted in the Camissa Footprint. A 'race-label' meaning 'mixed-race' in a lingo only understood against the Apartheid four-race silo lexicon replaced 400 years of history, heritage and struggles. The first people to experience dispossession as indigenes and slaves; the first to experience forced removals and wars involving land and cattle theft; the first people to experience pass laws; the first people to experience the brutality of torture and of genocide; and the first people to put up heroic resistance over a much longer and persistent period than any other community or set of communities in South Africa, should not have to continue to endure insult and continue to not be able to identify themselves and this amazing heritage. The term 'Coloured' does no justice to this Camissa heritage which I for one am proud of. It enhances my pride in being an African. It enhances my belonging to a diverse family of Southern African communities and when I say I am a South African it reminds me that this should never mean that I see this entity defined narrowly by the imperial-imposed borders or as a chauvinistic nation aggressive to others who don't fit narrow notions of South Africanness.

It is exactly because of our Camissa heritage that the Apartheid regime found it so hard to define the 'Coloured' box that they tried to herd us into. First in the Population Registration Act they said –

A white person is one who in appearance is, or who is generally accepted as, a white person, but does not include a person who although in appearance obviously a white person, is generally accepted as a coloured person. A native is a person who is in fact or is generally accepted as a member of any aboriginal race or tribe of Africa. A Coloured person is a person who is not a white person, nor a native. Every coloured person or every native whose name is so included shall be classified by the Director according to the ethnic or other group to which he belongs.

And in the Group Areas Act, they told us there will be:

A coloured group in which shall be included (i) any person who is not a member of the white group or of the native group; and (ii) any woman, to whichever race, tribe or class she may belong, between whom and a person who is, in terms of sub-paragraph (i), a member of the coloured group, there exists a marriage, or who cohabits with such a person;

They then too gave themselves the powers to declare groups, and proceeded to contradict their definition of Coloured and of Native by declaring the tribal organised Griqua, Nama and San to be Coloured. They also created 'Other Coloured' for the likes of some of us who were either too black or too white in appearance and 'Cape Malay', based on little more than the fact that these were slave descendants that were not Christian, but Muslim. When the ANC came to power they held on to the Apartheid 'Race-Silos' for dear life and even although they abolished the Population Registration Act of 1950 and the Group Areas Act of 1950, they kept alive the classification of this same weirdly concocted constructed identity. They also used it for discriminatory purposes as found by the Constitutional Court in 2016.

This is all part of our story and through telling it we pay tribute to our ancestral continuum and this underpins our identity – who we are.

Isn't the Camissa Footprint and all within this story a much more valuable and meaningful expression than 'Coloured'. It is a proud story of an African people who faced with overwhelming adversity, rose up above it and conquered that adversity.

Self-identity is an extremely important principle to which I subscribe. I believe that the state should have no role in identifying or categorizing people, racialising people and using this for social engineering purposes.

I say with pride I AM CAMISSA; I AM AFRICAN; I AM SOUTHERN AFRICAN and this is what I mean when I express pride as a South African. I am proud to have spent my life fighting this liberation struggle. Proudly Camissa. How could I ever be proud of a label like 'Other Coloured'?

© Patric Tariq Mellet

Editor's Note: South Africa may have started with the Khoena and San, but today consists of: Portuguese, English, French, Danish and Dutch, Germans, Ambonese, Malagasy, West African Bantu.

Slaves from African; Malagasy; Indian, Sri Lankan, Bangladeshi, Pakistani; and Southeast Asian (Indonesian, Myanmar, Thai, Vietnamese, Cambodian, Malaysian, South Chinese). Mazbiekers (Mozambique, Zimbabwe, Malawi). French Huguenots, Namaqua, the Korana, the Einiqua and the San- Indonesian exiles; Batavian Chinese exiles (Peranakan) and refugees from the Manillas.

St Helenians, Indians, BaTswana, Malawians, Mozambicans. West African Kru people (Kroomen) and East African Siddis; British and German poor settlers, Portuguese draft dodgers, Jews fleeing pograms and persecution, Palestinians, Turks, 'Prize Slaves' liberated from slaver vessels; African slave diaspora from the Caribbean and Americas, Japanese, Chinese and other seamen from a host of countries jumping ship.

South Africa's story of diversity continues to this day, as migrants, refugees, and travelers, continue to find safe haven in the Cape of Good Hope.

(With grateful thanks to Patric Mellet for keeping a running tab of the country's history)

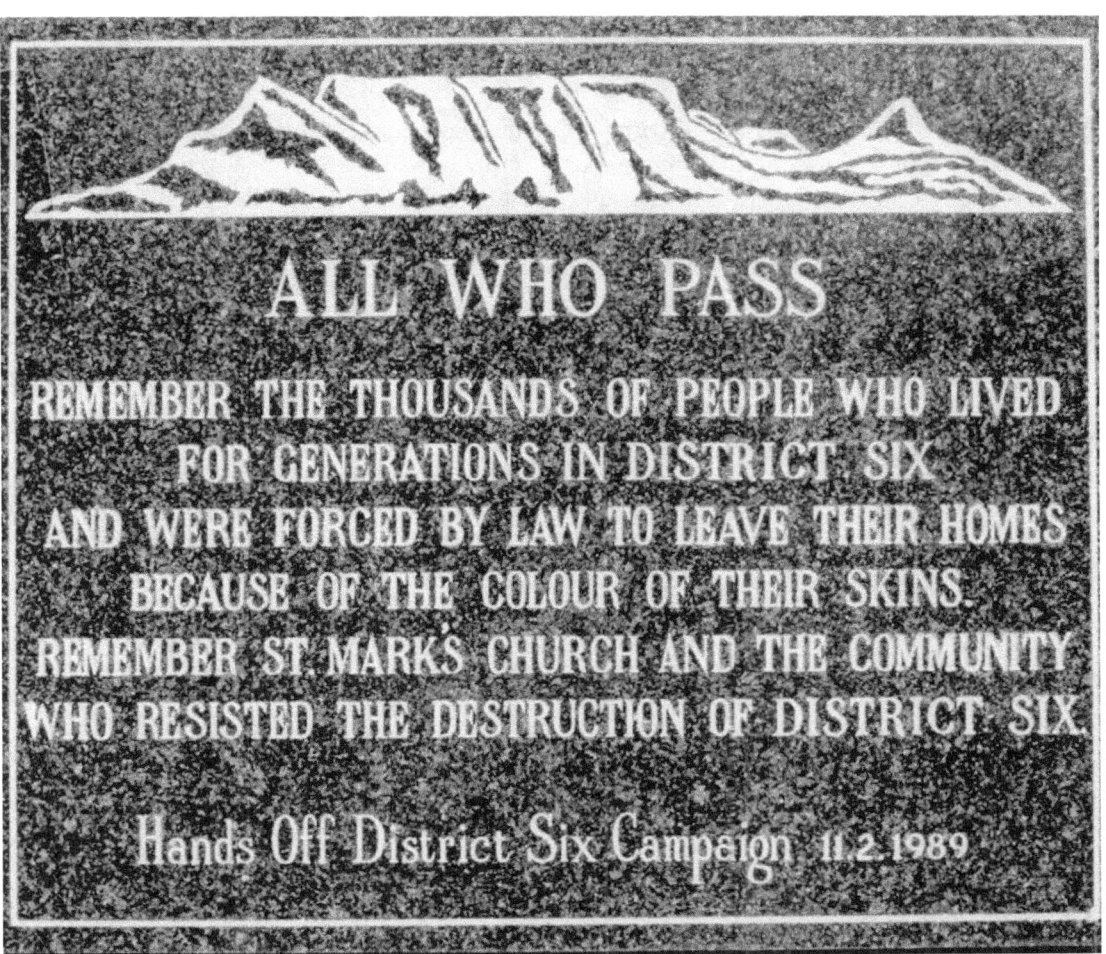

District Six Memory Plaque at the Moravian Church in District Six, Cape Town, South Africa. It commemorates the victims of apartheid-era forced removals through the racially divisive Group Areas Act. Photo by Henry Trotter, 2000

Islam 1-0-1

Post 9/11: The Religion of Peace

by Sharif Shah-Bilal

We have seen our bookstores flooded with many "experts" on Islam publishing their treatises - in a bid to inform the hitherto ignorant world as to what Islam actually amounts to. Many of these publications tend to waffle on and on without giving an objective insight to the religion and it's adherents.

There are so many in the media: - shock-jocks, talking heads pundits who frequently brand Islam as a front for terrorism, that we need to clarify - enlighten the world at large about what Islam stands for. The greatest jihad (struggle) is (by) the one who strives against his own self - his own weaknesses, desires, wants and failings. The very name Islam means religion of peace.

The term Islam is related to the Syriac 'aslem which means, "to make peace, surrender" and that in turn appears to be derived from the Semitic stem of *slem which means to be complete.

The Arabic term 'islam means "submission" and itself comes from the term 'aslama, which means, "to surrender, resign oneself." In Islam, the fundamental duty of each member is to submit to Allah (Arabic for "the God") and whatever Allah wants of them. A person who follows Islam is called a Muslim, and this means "one who surrenders to God."

We thus see that Islam is closely related to the Arabic word for peace, salaam. Muslims believe that true peace can only be achieved through true obedience to the will of Allah. Commitment to Islam is supposed to result in a constant struggle to achieve peace, justice and equality.

To facilitate a better simplified understanding of what it means to be a Muslim - compared to that portrayed in the mass hysterical rhetoric of the media; I have attempted to clarify some of the misconceptions by elaborating upon the complexities of the religion per sé and how it reveals itself to the adherents in various parts of the world.

(Certain instances of editorialising are mine...)

In order to become a Muslim, one is required to uphold the Five Pillars of Islam

SHAHADAH: Article of Faith - Declaration and belief in the Oneness of God and the finality of the prophet-hood of Muhammad

SALAH: Establishment of the five daily prayers (Fij'r, Zuhr, As'r, Maghrib and Isha)

ZAKAH: Concern for and almsgiving to the needy

SAWM: Self-purification through fasting during the month of Ramadhan

HAJJ: The pilgrimage to Makkah for those who are able - if he/she can afford it, if one is healthy and debt free.

First there is the Qu'ran ... from which comes Shariah - Islamic jurisprudence - usually under the unquestionable guidance of Jamaatul ... Islam whereupon the mufti's/mullah's sit on their thrones (they certainly act as if they are) as they are a law unto themselves - beyond reproach ... not unlike the Vatican and it's head.

True, the Sunni are those who fall under the Four Khalifa's - disciples of Prophet Muhammad. It is enough to uphold the five pillars of islam, to ensure one's entrance in Jannat ... heaven.

The tablighi's on the other hand, are those who claim to live by the Sunnah (examples) of Prophet Muhammad viz. Hadith. The Hadith ... a series of books containing the teachings, sayings and examples of Muhammad 's life -

Sunnah as exemplified [sic] by the tablighi's (those who practice Muhammad's example - who in turn go out and invite adherents who are possibly slacking in their religious duties - to return to performing the obligatory fives times a day salah - (prayers) amongst other things)

What has been done by the Tabligh Jammat ala taliban viz. Taqlif Jamaat (burdening throng - my personal name for them) - is to take certain examples from the hadith - interpret them and apply them as they see fit - not only to themselves, but to all Muslims - especially the less than regular five times salah adherers - especially those who seem to have totally forgone these prayers. They hope that by accusing those failing in their duties - the instilled guilt will shame them and provoke them to adhere more ardently.

As McCarthyism was to the usa, the KGB and other such strong-arm forces to those over whom they wielded power and fear - so are the aforementioned - tabligh/taliban to the Islamic world. It's all about subjugation - forcing everyone to toe the line - or else ...

Similarly; as we have many variances - schools of thought in Christianity; from Catholicism, to Anglican to Protestants and their respective offshoots; to charismatic preachers and televangelists, so do we find mirror examples within Islam. So, in the whole general scheme of things, Christian fundamentalists are no different to the fanatics of Islam, as both can be equally reprehensible ... as they try to impose their will - their brand of faith upon the whole world.

These are the thought police - spoken of in George Orwell's 1984 ...

So, what we usually have with taliban types - ummi - (illiterate) except for being Hafiz'ul'Qu'ran (one who can recite the Qu'ran off by heart) is a lowly educated clan of fanatics, (most of whom are unable to understand the Arabic meaning) who preach/admonish and intimidate an even more ummi-like populace into abject fear and compliance ...

Here is a clear example ...

We all know Islam to be a paternalistic religion; what with men being one level/step (or is it seven) above/ahead of their wives; but their

wives protectors none-the-less ...

Well, when Muhammad spoke of admonishing one's wife for such and such grievances, he suggested thrashing the wife with twenty/fifty - one hundred lashes as the infraction demanded. (It's in the Hadith ...)

But ... he went on to say that they should be beaten with the force, as if they were being struck with a woman's light headscarf.

Now tell me ... just where do the Taliban adhere to this continued piece of advice ... tradition from Prophet Muhammad???

What this boils down to is that they have taken out of the Hadith that which suits them, and applied it as they - in their omniscience/omnipotence see fit.

Woe behold anyone who tries to refute their authority ...

Within Islam - from Islam, we have several movements, of which I have listed the more prominent ones:

i) Sunni:followers of Prophet Muhammad and the four khalifa's (disciples of Muhammad)

ii) Shi'ite: followers of Hazrat Ali - Muhammad's grandson

iii) Ba'hai: yes an off-shoot from Islam (Shoghi Effendi, The Bap Ba'ha'ullah)

iv) Druze: Christian – although some of which are known to be Muslim

v) Sufi: mystics who come out of all the aforementioned

v) Ismaili/Khodja/Aga Khani, etc. - stemming from the Shia's

vi)   Nation of Islam ... as founded by Elijah Muhammad - primarily within the USA.

Back to Asia Minor and beyond ...

Together with Indonesia and Malaysia; the Middle East, Africa and USA, we have roughly 200 different nationalities, cultures - traditions - especially in Africa where we have some 150 plus languages with differing dialects and customs. Even with the intended aim of proposing and sustaining Arabic as the sole language of Islam, has somewhat fallen by the wayside, as the aforementioned complexities of one language, far supersedes - outweighs this ideal. Quite often, disparities between various Islamic groups are just as likely to cause friction, as their supposed differences compared to and within other religions of "the west".

(Just see how the Jan'jawi'id of Sudan (barbaric killers and terrorists) have waged heinious crimes - bordering on genocide; attacking, slaughtering elderly men, burning whole villages, raping women and children, forcing the youth into slavery - all this against their "African" Muslim brethren. No relationship between these barbaric terrorists and Islam is inferred.

Islam, as practiced throughout the world, is as varied, as are varieties of wines - to be savoured, enjoyed and preferred ...

When referring to the Arab world, most people automatically consider all predominately Muslim countries to be included - whether they attempt to isolate one particular region or not. Most people's knowledge of islam does not permit them to deal with the Arab/Muslim world in it's complexed, separate or entirely different entities require.

Given these parameters, it should be easier to understand why the whole Middle East/Asia Minor situation is not nearly as clear-cut as one would imagine. It has very little to do with the "Us vs. Them" syndrome.

Similarly, it is the misguided/misconstrued concept of 72 celestial virgins that is used by uneducated mufti's/mullahs upon hapless followers, That draws many into committing these often bizarre acts of suicide bombings - usually with innocent women and children becoming victims of their brazen acts of heroism.

Footnote:

The whole ridiculous "towel-head" stereotype is so far removed from reality, as gross ignorance will have it. It can never be stressed strongly enough, that not all turban wearers are necessarily connected to Islam, as many are Sikhs or any of the other branches of Vedanta/Hinduism. Many nationalities further east (totally unrelated to Islam or the Indo-Pak subcontinent) have turbans as part of their natural attire.

Have we heard of any clear explanation how or why 20,000 Muslims in Karachi alone - with similar cases in Malaysia and Indonesia where there has been rioting and clashing with their own governments? The media bias does not permit them to focus on this or clarify their own lack of knowledge/insight - instead choosing to spew rampant reports of disinformation concerning the whole situation - along with what it means to be Muslim vs. Arab vs. Terrorist ... None are synonymous with each other. Although secular Islam might be the preferred ideal - the many prevailing factors hardly make that a possibility - let alone a reality - an acceptable norm satisfying Western standards.

Of all the political organisations and groups, many of the new-grown terms; Fedda'yin, Hamas, Muja'haddin, Wa'habi, Jihadist, Islamist, and other splinter group labels have been erroneously applied to Muslims across the board. These have very little - if anything to do with the true tenements of Islam.

Over the past 20 years, we have seen growing numbers of dissatisfied Muslims break with tradition - fundamentalist Islam and seek alternative paths towards their own spirituality - whether it be other "sects" within Islam or various off-shoots thereof - that we constantly hear narrow-minded fundamentalists voicing criticisms or condemnation for what has become branded as shirk or murtad "drifters" who are branded enemies of Islam and therefore liable to have fatwah's passed on them ... condemning them to death.

Again, we have clear examples of these same "scary" attitudes stemming from within mainstream Christianity. It helps very little to get carried away by branding everyone with the same brush, attaching the same label to such a diverse people - not knowing from whence they originated - let alone what exactly many stand for.

Both Christianity and Islam have their strong points - valuable to sincere adherents. Both Islam and Christianity have their failings - equally questionable and in some cases reprehensible to those who follow - are led as gullible sheep - in blind faith.

(c) Owen Greenland.2003

Notes from the
Wild Side

By Mandy Tomson

OSCAR –
THE NOT SO FINAL CHAPTER

The protracted process of bringing Oscar Pistorius to book is finally almost over. And few South Africans have faith that either truth or justice was manifest in the result. A mere six years of which Pistorius will serve approximately three – leaving him with roughly four years of total time served for killing a young woman. There are people who commit unintentional vehicular homicide who serve more time and the state is appealing the sentence.

There remain some critical unanswered questions that gnaw at many observers. Everyone has a narrative and this is my deduction, based on Oscar's own testimony:

Twas the evening before Valentine's Day and Reeva Steenkamp had gone shopping in order to prepare a special meal for Oscar. He surfed cars and porn on the internet upstairs while she prepared the meal in the kitchen downstairs. She called him when it was ready and served him a romantic, candle-lit dinner. He was evidently not in a particularly romantic mood because as soon as they finished the meal, he went upstairs and continued surfing the internet and watching television while she cleaned up. This beautiful woman then joined him in his bedroom and did yoga poses next to the bed in shorty shorts while he began to doze off.

This would have been disappointing to most women, having made an effort to have a romantic evening in a relatively new relationship. She may have tried to let it go in the interests of harmony as many women do – especially if he had a sore shoulder as he claimed and since there was always the following evening on actual Valentine's day.

It was a warm evening and the sliding doors to the balcony were open with fans placed to facilitate the flow of fresh air. Oscar was already falling asleep and asked Reeva to bring in the fans and close the sliding doors before she went to sleep. In the early hours of the morning, he woke up to discover that she had failed to honour his request. As a self-confessed vulnerable, disabled man with anxiety who was concerned about South Africa's high crime, he must have been irritated. After all, there had been a recent burglary a few houses away. He had also woken up against his will – after all, everyone wants an uninterrupted night's sleep.

I suspect these facts provoked an argument and neighbours testified that they heard raised voices. Their evidence was discounted due to some minor contradictions in timing and the possibility that they mistook Oscar's high-pitched screams for a woman's voice.

Nevertheless, Oscar's version is that he had a short, cute, sleepy verbal exchange with Reeva, and then got out of bed – on his stumps – to close the sliding doors and bring in the fans while she went to the bathroom without him noticing. If everything was harmonious between them, why didn't Reeva bring in the fans and close the doors? We saw how unstable he is on his stumps and she certainly knew, so why would she not insist that he stay in bed while she brings in the fans and closes the sliding doors?

Oscar managed to not notice that she left the room and she didn't just close the door to the toilet cubicle but also locked it and was in possession of her cell phone. Why? Was he in the habit of barging into the tiny cubicle while she did her business? Since we now know she was the source of the noise, Oscar could not have perceived any danger until she arrived in the bathroom and made said noise. So why did she already have her phone with her? He was already awake so she there was no reason why she could not use her phone in the bedroom for fear of waking him up.

What is fascinating is that Oscar who was vulnerable and paranoid about crime heard a "strange noise" but chose not to make use of the alarm system and panic button for which he paid substantial money to protect himself. Instead, he chose to arm himself and run toward the "danger" while at his most vulnerable – on his stumps.

While running down the passage toward the bathroom with his gun, he managed

to retain enough rationality to assess that a warning shot might end up ricocheting and hurting him – but that he might kill a human by firing his gun four times into an enclosed space somehow eluded him.

The only way Judge Masipa's verdict of culpable homicide could be sustained is if Oscar thought he was shooting at an animal that had invaded the bathroom.

What is far more plausible is that they had an argument, he lost his temper and she fled to the bathroom with her phone and locked herself in the toilet.

In his interview with ITV, he not so subtly blamed Reeva: if only she had told him she was going to the bathroom. Who does such a thing? Why would someone inform their partner they are going to the bathroom? If only she had "answered" him after he claimed he asked her to call the police.

His explanation of the shooting is so preposterous that many people, including myself, remain convinced it was dolus directus – he executed Reeva. Thanks to a rigorous defence, he was ultimately convicted of dolus eventualis; thanks to an irrational and sympathetic judge, he was sentenced with a stump discount. One can only feel gratitude that our constitution allows the state to appeal.

AH, RUGBY!

I could not watch rugby during the apartheid years because I felt it was the sport of the ruling class and was instinctively repulsed. Having returned to post-apartheid South Africa from the US eight years ago, I became a convert, attracted to the fast and relentless nature of the sport – especially in contrast to American football where play occurs in three to six second increments before everyone stops for a coffee, a consultation and a change of personnel. All these gorgeous rugby players, dreadlocks flying, certainly helped my positive re-evaluation of the sport.

This is the first SuperRugby season that I couldn't give a shit and I have tried to analyse why:

1) There are too many teams of radically different abilities which has created mismatched contests that turn into one-sided massacres. I am not referring to the Argentinian Jaguares or the Japanese Sunwolves since there is a long-term logic to their inclusion in the SuperRugby tournament: Argentina and Japan are keen rugby nations whose level of play cannot advance until their players are included in an annual tournament that tests their skills against the best in the world. However, it is clear that Australia and South Africa need to each drop a team. The conference system is too unwieldy and uncompetitive.

2) The departure of Boots and All: I consider myself fairly well-informed. I read newspapers and news online and I watch television news on a variety of different channels. However, I had no idea Boots and All had been cancelled. I tuned in on Thursday night at the beginning of the SuperRugby season – nothing. I googled it and discovered it had been cancelled and replaced by two shows called TMO First Half and TMO Second Half; I don't know their broadcast times but I do know that random glances at the television program frequently have the Second Half airing before the First Half. No one I know watches either show. Boots and All had been the rugby show around which all English speakers gathered, a unifying point for us rugby fans who would discuss the show

and the assorted opinions expressed on it. What sane television producer cancels a successful show with a brand name and a known timeslot and changes both the timeslot and the name and divides the show into two?!

3) The departure of familiar names: rugby players have always tended to leave SA, especially toward the end of their careers, but the collapse of the rand has enticed players to move overseas far earlier in their careers. Instead of a few new players being integrated into teams every year, it feels like an annual near-wholescale change of personnel that leaves one emotionally disconnected while watching a bunch of strangers.

4) Our 19th century coaching methods: there were two little off-field nuggets of information that emerged from the 2015 Rugby World Cup which told me that Springbok coach Heyneke Meyer was simply backwards: Springbok number eight Duane Vermeulen was asked what he thought of his opposite number in an upcoming match; looking almost bewildered, he dismissed the question, responding that the Boks don't focus on their opponents and simply go out and play their game; and a Springbok back was interviewed and admitted that Meyer had told them a year prior not to bother practicing quick offloads since that wasn't part of the game plan. Yes, we were beaten by Japan whose team members spend half their lives on their i-pads, researching the opposition.

Discouraging the practice of quick offloads is akin to a tennis coach instructing his player not to bother practicing volleys because the game plan is baseline play. That it may be, but to not practice volleys would limit the player's ability to exploit opportunities as they present themselves. Now we have Alastair Coetzee: I wish him the best but his record at the Stormers does not inspire confidence.

Johan Ackerman is clearly doing a fantastic job with the Lions and represents South Africa's most proven and successful coach in terms of guiding our rugby into the 21st century. However, there is one nugget of information that made me shake my head: the Lions pray together – before a match, after a match, in general… This is absolutely unacceptable. It is time that South African rugby abandoned the Christian culture that appears to infest most teams. Religion and business do not belong together and to create a team culture that depends on everyone being Christian is a dangerous precedent. How would a Muslim Sonny Bill Williams fit into a team like that? The most important guarantee of religious freedom is a secular government, secular business and secular education. We are a diverse nations of atheists, Wiccans, Muslims, Christians, Catholics, Jews, etc. A place of employment should focus on the skills necessary for the job and leave religion or the lack of it to the private sphere.

THE OLYMPICS

There were no catastrophes at the Rio Games but the biggest disappointment was the empty seats – even at marquee events such as swimming, gymnastics and track and field that are usually sold out.

It seems clear that hosting the Olympics has become too expensive and burdensome. An elegant solution would be to only accept bids from two neighbouring countries – that way, the costs for each would be halved; new infrastructure could be shared, lessening the chances of leftover, white-elephant facilities; and enhanced transportation connections between the neighbouring countries would prove to be of lasting benefit.

Caster Semenya's victory in the 800 metres was virtually guaranteed. It left many with an uneasy feeling. In 2010, after Semenya was reportedly required to take testosterone suppressants in order to be allowed to compete, her race times dropped. In 2015, the system was challenged by another athlete and the Court for the Arbitration of Sport ruled that the issue required more study because natural testosterone levels among men and women sometimes overlap and athletes shouldn't be forced to take testosterone suppressants. Since then, Semenya's race times bounced back to unbeatable levels.

This is an enormously complex issue. Certain body types are conducive to certain sports: you cannot be a short basketball player or a tall jockey, and the most talented athletes obviously have a massive physiological advantage over the rest of us. How does one determine what constitutes unfair versus natural advantage?

Constitutional law expert, Professor Pierre de Vos, believes Semenya has been targeted because her "gift comes in a package that disturbs stereotypical assumptions about women…" However, this is an oversimplification: Testosterone is considered performance-enhancing and if male and female athletes' biological passports show a sudden spike in their typical testosterone levels, they will be investigated for doping.

Let's review the unpleasant events that led us to this point.

The Semenya controversy exploded at the 2009 IAAF world championships. Then head of Athletics South Africa (ASA), Leonard Chuene, was exposed as a liar, embarrassing the country and also revealing Semenya to be partly complicit in the Berlin debacle and its aftermath, an issue ignored by the South African media.

After ASA depicted her as an innocent naïf who had never been gender-tested, the public had to process the shocking revelations that gender tests were conducted, the results were unfavourable, and she and Chuene knew about them before the race. Her victory became tainted with unease – her image as a victim clouded by the distasteful realization that she had remained silent amid an avalanche of lies.

Ironically, ASA and the ANC's actions throughout reflected the traditionally conservative refusal to tolerate any individuality in gender identity and sexual preference – men are men, women are women, and anyone else is a freak, so stop trying to classify "our girl" as a freak. ASA duped Semenya into gender tests requested by the IAAF. She was told they were drug tests because Chuene admittedly found the whole subject embarrassing and the very notion of intersex inconceivable. Semenya was not concealing a penis – end of story. She realised she was being gender-tested because – memo to genius Chuene – no "drug test" involves putting your feet in stirrups. Thanks to this dishonesty and culture of denial, the teenager was deprived of the psychological support that is supposed to accompany gender-testing and dispatched to Berlin intellectually and emotionally unprepared. Nevertheless, she understood, reluctantly or not, that the issue was unfair advantage, having already suffered years of hostile questions about her gender at local athletic meets.

When the preliminary gender-test results prompted the team doctor to recommend Semenya be withdrawn, Chuene faced a crisis: Exposing his own deceit would demonstrate that the gender tests were conducted without Semenya's informed consent, prohibiting the IAAF from using them to withdraw her or strip her of any medal. Since Semenya was legally entitled to run and emotionally unprepared for the test results, Chuene could have withheld them from her and privately fallen on his sword to the IAAF, pledging to redo the tests properly after the competition.

Alternatively, Chuene could have fallen on his sword to Semenya, but withdrawn her from the race because unfair advantage existed according to the rules at the time, her competitors suspected it, and the issue was not going away. He could have announced she was injured, allowing her to quietly retreat for counselling, treatment and re-testing. An understandably hurt, angry Semenya might have privately complained to the IAAF about Chuene's gender-test deception or sought compensation from ASA, but her departure from the competition would have defused her gender as an issue and helped protect her privacy.

Chuene combined the worst of both options: He told Semenya about the unfavourable test results and asked her to withdraw, traumatising the teen who cried, insisted she was a girl and begged to run; having implicated her in knowledge of her own unfair advantage, he then allowed her to run while he blew off the media and the IAAF with a torrent of lies and implausible denials. Whether by tacit or explicit trade-off, Semenya cooperated with Chuene's post-race cover-up by remaining silent.

Chuene brazenly denied ever receiving

a gender-test request from the IAAF, let alone having tests conducted. He protested that if Semenya was "European," she would be getting therapy for all this stress – a gratuitous racial embellishment given that it was his own dishonesty that had already deprived her of the timely counselling recommended by the IAAF. Actually, if Semenya was from a more compassionate, reality-based culture, she probably would have received medical and psychological assessments when she was much younger, rather than suffering humiliating, informal gynaecological inspections in school bathrooms at local athletic meets.

Chuene, however, portrayed formal gender testing as a morally degenerate Western human-rights violation when the harsh truth is that if Semenya looked traditionally feminine and was beaten by a manly-looking competitor from another country, ASA would have bayed for gender testing and Julius Malema would have complained that "our girl" was robbed by "a man." Chuene vowed that no gender testing ever had been or would be performed on Semenya. She would be kept out of competition – stuck in professional limbo amid ongoing personal innuendo – while ASA used her as a poster child to lobby the United Nations against gender testing.

This spectacular dishonesty was compounded by ignorant and misled ANC opportunists who railed on as though no intersex human had ever been born, no black athlete or official had ever questioned Semenya's gender, and no white athlete had ever been gender-tested – when gender-testing arose because of masculine whites from the former Soviet Union and East Germany who were either testosterone-pumped females, intersex or males passing as females. The excruciating nadir was Malema getting cheap laughs by pointing out that Semenya's parents were the ultimate gynaecological authority, having checked her vagina at birth. The ANC would stand tall against Western culturally imperialistic babble about gender ambiguity, and proudly stick to its own medical science wherein all humans are born with perfectly functioning organs in standard quantity, combination, location and hormone levels.

South Africa's sudden "principled" opposition to gender testing and wild accusations of racism ignited the media's suspicions and resolve. Given that doctors, nurses, friends, officials and coaches knew gender tests had already been conducted and there were multiple email exchanges, the cover-up was doomed from the start.

Semenya inevitably kept the gold because ASA violated medical ethics and IAAF protocol by conning her into the gender tests – never mind that she knew she was being conned. This lack of consent muddied what would otherwise have been a simple conspiracy to defy the rules for unfair advantage, akin to concealing the positive results of a drug test by claiming the test was never requested or conducted. The twisted irony is that Semenya's victory was deviously enabled by the very denial and cruelty that torment intersex, transgender, gay and lesbian South Africans.

The bottom-line for Semenya's competitors is that they lost thousands of Euros and title prestige in a contest with an athlete who knew she was not supposed to be running. The bottom-line for Semenya appears to be that she won, and she reportedly gained defiant emotional strength from watching replays of her victory. The tragedy she has yet to face is that the crude cover-up not only tarnished her image, but by blowing her confidentiality and preventing her from quietly exiting and then re-entering the sport – as in other cases involving intersex athletes – it undermined all her achievements up to and including Berlin as "pre-treatment." In the eyes of the world, she was starting over, this time on a level playing field, and the fact that her race times dropped seemed to prove prior unfair advantage.

Although Semenya comes from a conservative, rural culture that nurtured her vulnerability and defensive denial, she was no illiterate who recently fell off a turnip truck and then outran it in front of an athletics recruiter. She was a university student who knew that she was subject to all IAAF rules – like her peers – and that disapproval of a sport's rules is not grounds for breaking them. She also had the emotional support and moral example of ASA coach, Wilfred Daniels, who resigned in public protest of Chuene's dishonesty. Still Semenya chose to remain silent, seemingly oblivious to the collateral damage suffered by others: She never reached out to her competitors; she stayed clear of her peers' efforts to rescue ASA; she expressed no regret that her country's leaders were duped into lying on her behalf and that journalists were defamed as liars and racists; and she sought no broader meaning or solidarity with other intersex victims of persecution and African women suffering "corrective" rape because men deem them insufficiently feminine.

The only way Semenya's ongoing passivity could be excused was via the patronising narrative that this "poor girl" from "a small village" didn't understand and could not have been expected to comprehend sophis-

ticated, urban concepts such as rules and honesty, and therefore should not be held to the same standards as others, including Africans. This morally muddy ode to inequality does not generate respect or make her a marketable role model.

Semenya then appeared on television, bemoaning her finances and lack of sponsors, and her supporters launched a R1 million fundraising drive – just over a year after she pocketed close to a million from her victory plus a house reportedly built for her by the ANC Youth League. These donations further divided her from her peers who had to depend on their own merits, marketability and sensible money management.

So far, no lessons appear to have resonated from this dreadful saga – for Semenya, the nation or the ANC. Outdoing even Chuene's infantile incompetence, a post-Berlin report to parliament, paid for by we the people, helpfully referred to Semenya as "Mr. C. Semenye."

Semenya has never taken responsibility for her participation in the 2009 cover-up. She has never discussed any of these issues openly nor has she challenged the cruel cultural prejudices that birthed this ASA-orchestrated fiasco and that endanger not just the careers but the lives of Africans born with gender ambiguity.

The truth will set you free, Caster.